Looking
UP

When Life Gets You
DOWN

Other Selected Titles by Warren W. Wiersbe

Looking
UP

When Life Gets You
DOWN

WARREN W. WIERSBE

BakerBooks

a division of Baker Publishing Group
Grand Rapids, Michigan

Published by Baker Books
a division of Baker Publishing Group
P.O. Box 6287, Grand Rapids, MI 49516-6287
www.bakerbooks.com

Original edition published in 1984 by Revell under the title *Why Us? When Bad Things Happen to God's People*

Printed in the United States of America

Library of Congress Cataloging-in-Publication Data
Wiersbe, Warren W.
    Looking up when life gets you down / Warren W. Wiersbe.
        p.   cm.
    Rev. ed. of: Why us?
    ISBN 978-0-8010-1405-5 (pbk.)
    1. Suffering—Religious aspects—Christianity. 2. Theodicy. 3. Consolation.
4. Christian life. I. Wiersbe, Warren W. Why us? II. Title.
BV4909.W53 2012
248.8´6—dc23   2012000562

12   13   14   15   16   17   18   7   6   5   4   3   2   1

Contents

Preface to the New Edition

This book was originally published in 1984 at a time when some people were promoting "process theology" and its collateral idea of a "limited God." Their argument was that things are bad because God is too weak to do better. When He gets stronger, things will improve, and we help Him get stronger as we overcome our trials.

Today, neither of these ideas takes up much space on the theological agenda, but the major question is still with us: Why do bad things happen to seemingly innocent people? Other questions stem from this one, including: Why is there so much suffering in this world? Is God limited in what He can do? Doesn't He know our pains and disappointments? If He does know, does He really care? Dedicated Christians who seek to please and glorify the Lord ask these questions, and also children who don't even understand what's happening. Costly natural disasters like floods, fires, and oil spills are still in the news, along with wretched economic conditions that wipe out savings, threaten retirements, and destroy jobs. These calamities touch the lives of millions of hardworking people who, from a human point of view, don't seem to deserve them. Even the most devout Christian people occasionally wonder what the Lord is doing.

Helen Keller wrote in her book *Optimism*: "Although the world is full of suffering, it is full also with the overcoming of it." Blind and deaf since childhood, she became an overcomer and encouraged others to overcome. "Man is born broken," says one of the characters in Eugene O'Neill's play *The Great God Brown*. "He lives by mending. The grace of God is glue."

The grace of God! That's the answer God gave the apostle Paul when three times he asked God to remove his pain. "My grace is sufficient for you, for my power is made perfect in weakness" (2 Cor. 12:9). In his poem "The Light of the Stars," Longfellow wrote, "Know how sublime a thing it is to suffer and be strong." If we experience more suffering, James 4:6 assures us that God "gives us more grace."

It is also by the grace of God that I hold to the orthodox Christian position that God is sovereign. For reasons known only to Him, He is using the difficulties of life to accomplish His purposes. The Lord has not abandoned us. He has provided in His Word truths that can strengthen and encourage us, and it is these truths I have tried to share in this book.

During our years of ministry, my wife and I have prayed, wept, and counseled with many hurting people and have had our own share of painful disappointments. But we have always found the Lord to be a caring and comforting heavenly Father who gives us what we need just when we need it. From my reading of the Bible, biography and autobiography, and my personal contacts with many of God's finest servants, I have learned that the most exemplary and effective people of faith have suffered greatly and yet have triumphed to the glory of the Lord. Their burdens and battles haven't ruined them; they have made them what they are.

The aims of this book are to answer some questions about God and suffering in this world and to point to faith in the grace and power of God as our greatest help when we hurt. In short, it aims to help you look up when life gets you down. If you don't think you need God's help today, perhaps you will tomorrow, or perhaps you can help someone else. Compassionate Christians minimize their own pain as they emphasize encouraging others who suffer and need God's help. To receive a blessing from God is wonderful; but to *be* a blessing from God is even greater. May sharing the truths in this book help us all to be a blessing to hurting people.

I don't send out this book from an isolated ivory tower but from the trenches where the battle still goes on. May what I share encourage you to be happy with the will of God and strengthened to do His will and minister to others. The best is yet to come!

Warren W. Wiersbe

To You Who Hurt

Be kind, for everyone you meet is fighting a battle."

I'm not certain who first made that statement, but it gives wise counsel indeed. All of us are fighting battles and carrying burdens, and we desperately need all the help we can get. The last thing any of us needs is for somebody to add to our problems.

It isn't the normal demands of life that break us; it's the painful surprises. We find ourselves fighting battles in a war we never declared, and carrying burdens for reasons we don't understand. I'm not talking about "reaping what we sow," because most of us are smart enough to know when and why that happens. If we break the rules, we have to accept the consequences; but sometimes things happen even when we *don't* break the rules.

When life hands us these painful surprises, we start to ask questions. We wonder if perhaps we've been cheated. We begin to doubt that life makes any sense at all. Bad things *do* happen

11

to God's people; and when these bad things happen, our normal response is to ask, "Why us?"

This book is one man's effort to try to help the many people who are hurting, people who, in their pain, are asking fundamental questions that get down to the foundations of life. Is there a God? If there is, what kind of God is He? By what rules is He running the game of life? Is He free, or is He handcuffed by His own universe? Is He working out a plan, or is He so limited that He can't intervene in the affairs of life? Does it do any good to pray? Do we have any authoritative information *from* God and *about* God, or must we settle for our own limited conclusions, based on bits and pieces collected from the shattered experiences of life?

These are important questions and they must be answered.

This book is part of what Mortimer Adler would call "the Great Conversation," that fascinating discussion that has been going on for centuries, wherever men and women have pondered the problem of evil in this world. My hope is to help people who hurt and who are perplexed by the problems of life.

For more than sixty years, I have been involved in Christian ministry, trying to help people draw upon the vast spiritual resources God makes available to us. I have had to ask some fundamental questions. Have I been applying the right medicine to the right maladies? Has my diagnosis of the situation been correct? How much do I really know about the God I've been preaching and writing about all these years? Do I have the kind of faith that works in the battlefield of life?

As I wrestled with these and other questions, I came to some conclusions that will be elaborated on in the chapters of this book. But, just so you know where we are heading, here they are.

1. *Our answers to the problem of suffering must have intellectual integrity.* We are made in the image of God, and this means we must think. We must ask the right questions if we hope to get the right answers. This means we must all become philosophers and question our questions. We can't avoid this, because the minute you try to answer a question about life, you become a philosopher.

2. *People live by promises, not by explanations.* This is the balance to number one. Nobody can fully answer all the questions; but, even if we could, the answers are not guaranteed to make life easier or suffering more bearable. God is not standing at the end of a syllogism, nor is peace of mind found at the conclusion of an argument. In every area of life there must always be an element of faith—marriage, business, science, and ordinary everyday decisions. What you believe determines how you behave, but you can't always *explain* what you believe and why you believe it. "Faith is one of the forces by which men live," wrote Henry James, "and the total absence of it means collapse."

3. *We must live!* Life is a gift from God, and we must treasure it, protect it, and invest it. We may be able to postpone some decisions, but *we cannot postpone living.* "Life cannot wait until the sciences may have explained the universe scientifically," wrote José Ortega y Gasset. "We cannot put off living until we are ready. . . . Life is fired at us point-blank." Either we come to grips with life and make it work the best we can, or we give up. The ultimate in giving up is suicide. The most important question in life is not "Why do bad things happen to good people?" but, "Why are people here at all?" What is the purpose of life? Does anybody know?

4. *We must live for others.* Suffering can make us selfish or sacrificing. It can make us a part of the problem or a part of the answer. Cardinal John Henry Newman's friend John Keble used to say, "When you find yourself overpowered as it were by melancholy, the best way is to go out and do something kind to somebody or other." Good advice! The apostle Paul explained to the suffering people of his day that God "comforts us in all our troubles, so that we can comfort those in any trouble with the comfort we ourselves have received from God" (2 Cor. 1:4). We were created, I think, to be channels and not reservoirs, to think of others and not only ourselves.

5. *The resources for creative suffering are available to us.* All of nature depends on "hidden resources," and so must we. Human history sparkles with the testimonies of people who could have been victims but who decided to be victors. Suffering will be either your master or your servant, depending on how you handle the crises of life. After all, a crisis doesn't make a person; it reveals what a person is made of. What life does to us depends on what life finds in us. The resources are available if we will only use them.

As we consider these matters, we will have to stretch our minds and do some serious thinking. At the same time, we must open our hearts to the kind of spiritual truths that can't be examined in the laboratory or manipulated by a computer. But above all else, we must be willing to obey truth wherever it leads us. It is not enough for your mind to be enlightened, or your heart enriched; your will must be enabled in the service of others. Suffering is not a topic for speculation; it is an

opportunity for compassion and involvement. The mind grows
by taking in, but the heart grows by giving out.

"He is already half false who speculates on truth and does
not do it," said F. W. Robertson, who knew what it was to suffer
and to die young. "Truth is given, not to be contemplated, but
to be done. Life is an action—not a thought."

But if action is to be intelligent, it must begin with thought.

Our first responsibility, then, is to try to answer "The Really
Big Question."

The Really Big Question

Why do bad things happen to good people?

You may not realize it, but when you ask that question, you are revealing a great deal about what you believe. Behind that question is a set of assumptions that you believe to be true and by which you manage your life. Each of us has a personal "statement of faith," and it is revealed by the questions we ask.

Everybody believes something about the universe, life, death, happiness, God, goodness, evil, and other people. These beliefs are like the axioms in geometry: they are difficult to prove, but if you reject them, you can't solve the problems. "It is strictly impossible to be a human being," wrote Aldous Huxley, "and not to have views of some kind about the universe at large."

What assumptions lie behind the question, "Why do bad things happen to good people?"

To begin with, in asking this question we are assuming that *there are values in life*. Some things are "good" and some things are "bad." For centuries, philosophers have discussed the meaning of "goodness" and "what the good life is," and they don't always agree. But this much is sure: you and I would rather have the "good life" than suffer from the "bad things" that can happen to us. We would rather have good health than sickness, good success in business than failure, good times and not sorrow.

There is another assumption behind our question: we are assuming that *there is order in the universe*. We assume that there is *a cause* for the "bad things" that happen in people's lives. When tragedy occurs, we say, "Look, there's something wrong here. This should never have happened." Our protest tells people that we believe in an orderly universe, one that "makes sense." Such things as the birth of a stillborn child, or the murder of a lovely bride, seem out of place to us.

A third assumption is that *people are important*. Few of us ever ask whether bad things happen to tulips, guppies, or rabbits. No doubt they do, but our great concern is people. We assume that people are different from plants and animals, and that this difference is important.

Our fourth assumption is, I think, rather obvious: we believe that *life is worth living*. After all, if life is *not* worth living, why bother to ask questions at all? Why not just end it all? Albert Camus stated it bluntly: "There is but one truly serious philosophical problem, and that is suicide. Judging whether life is or is not worth living amounts to answering the fundamental question of philosophy." The fact that we are wrestling with these problems is evidence that we think life is worth living, that we are not (to use comedian Fred Allen's phrase) "on a treadmill to oblivion."

We can add a fifth assumption: we believe that *we are capable of finding some answers and profiting from them.* We assume that we are rational people with minds that work, and that the rational universe around us will offer some answers. We may not be able to understand and explain everything, but we will learn enough that we will be encouraged to face the struggles of life and keep going. Built into this assumption is the belief that we are free to ask questions and pursue truth. We are not robots.

If, then, you are sincerely asking, "Why do bad things happen to good people?" this is what you believe:

- There are values in this universe.
- The universe is logical and orderly.
- People are important.
- Life is really worth living.
- We can find answers that will help us.

But merely stating our assumptions doesn't instantly solve our problems. In fact, these assumptions help to create a whole new series of questions that we dare not avoid. If there *are* values in the universe, where did they come from? What makes "good" good and "bad" bad? If the universe is rational and orderly, and we can understand cause and effect, how did it get that way? If people are different from plants and animals, what made the difference? And why are people important? What is it about life that makes it worth living?

I think that all of these important questions can be summed up in what I think is the biggest question of all: *What is the purpose of life?* If I know who I am, why I am here, and how I fit into the scheme of the universe, then I can better understand and handle the difficult experiences of life. As Nietzsche wrote, "If we have our own *why* of life, we shall get along with almost any *how*." Or, as the Roman proverb puts it, "When the pilot does not know what port he is heading for, no wind is the right wind."

So, the really big question is not, "Why do bad things happen to good people?" but "What is the purpose of life?" We can't honestly answer the first question until we answer the second. Unless we know the purpose of life, we can't determine what experiences are "good" and what experiences are "bad."

A beautiful Old Testament story illustrates this. Joseph's brothers were jealous of him and hated him, so they sold him into slavery. Joseph's father, Jacob, thought that his beloved son was dead; but actually Joseph was a slave in Egypt. He spent several trying years in prison, but then, by a series of wonderful circumstances, Joseph was made second ruler of the land. As the result of this, he was able to protect his father and brothers during a terrible famine (see Genesis 37–50).

From our human perspective, what happened to Joseph was "bad." Jealousy and hatred are bad. It is a bad thing to be separated from your aged father and sold as a slave. It is a bad thing to be falsely accused and thrown into prison. But, in the end, all of these events worked out for good. Joseph said to his brothers, "You intended to harm me, but God intended it for good to accomplish what is now being done, the saving of many lives" (Gen. 50:20).

In other words, we had better be cautious in identifying the experiences of life as "good" or "bad," because we might be wrong! The Christian believer holds on to Romans 8:28, "And we know that in all things God works for the good of those who love him, who have been called according to his purpose."

But what is the purpose of life?

Many people sincerely believe that *happiness* is the purpose of life. I'm not talking about pleasure seekers who live only to "eat, drink, and be merry." Rather, I'm referring to decent people who simply want to enjoy companionship and love, earn a living, pay their bills, perhaps raise a family, and have a share in the "good things" of life.

I may be wrong, but it seems to me that happiness is not the major goal of life, but instead is a wonderful byproduct. Most of the people I know who have made happiness their goal have ended up miserable! But the people who have invested their lives in worthwhile pursuits have discovered a measure of happiness. As we mature in life, our ideas of happiness change; and often with this maturity comes a deeper understanding of sorrow.

Making happiness your goal in life could bring in an element of selfishness as well. *My* happiness might turn out to be *your sorrow!*

Whatever purpose motivates your life, it must be something big enough and grand enough to make the investment worthwhile. Life is too short, and too difficult, to waste on trivialities. "Many persons have a wrong idea of what constitutes true happiness," wrote Helen Keller in her journal. "It is not attained through self-gratification but through fidelity to a worthy purpose."

It is my conviction that life is worth living, in spite of the problems and difficulties, because man is involved in such a "worthy purpose." Bertrand Russell called man "a curious accident in a backwater," and cynical H. L. Mencken called man "a local disease of the cosmos." But man bears the image of God and was created to share the glory of God. The old catechism states this "worthy purpose" beautifully: "Man was created to glorify God and to enjoy Him forever."

The prophet Isaiah had this same purpose in mind when he wrote: "Bring my sons from afar and my daughters from the ends of the earth—everyone who is called by my name, whom I created for my glory, whom I formed and made" (Isa. 43:6–7).

Bad things not only happen to *good* people, but they also happen to a select group of "good people"—*God's* people. The fact that we know God as our Father and Jesus Christ as our Savior doesn't exempt us from the normal burdens of life, or from those special trials that surprise us at times. In fact, our faith could even make us a special target for enemy attack.

The five assumptions that we discussed earlier seem to give evidence to the reality of God in this universe. It is God who has put values into the universe and who determines what is "good" and what is "bad." It is God who made man and gave man his important place in creation. It is God who maintains order in the universe, even when you and I conclude that something has gone wrong. It is God who makes life worth living.

There are those who would substitute "evolution" for God. But if the purpose of life is to fulfill evolutionary progress, then "bad things" can't happen to anybody. In fact, we can't even use the words "bad" and "good" because whatever is supposed to occur in the evolutionary process is good. The tragedies of life are only helping to lift man higher on the evolutionary scale. Furthermore, man is no longer important for himself, but only as he contributes to the "long, slow evolutionary process."

I seriously doubt if many people ever found comfort in sorrow or strength in pain by believing this. Such ideas are fine for the laboratory or the ivory tower, but they lose their vitality in an intensive care ward or beside an open grave.

Furthermore, while evolution might help to explain birth defects and other physical problems, it can never explain the existence of *moral* evil in this world. It is one thing if your daughter is born with some defect, but quite something else if she is kidnapped, raped, and murdered. Are those wicked deeds also a part of the "long, slow evolutionary process"? Is the man who would do such deeds really a guilty criminal, or is he only an agent in evolutionary progress?

I am not suggesting that when we bring God into the discussion we automatically solve all the problems. In fact, we introduce some new problems, as we shall see in later chapters. But I am affirming that to leave God out of the discussion is to make the discussion unnecessary. We have problems with evil in this world, not because of our unbelief, but because of our faith!

The great British Bible teacher Dr. G. Campbell Morgan said it this way:

> Men of faith are always the men that have to confront problems. Blot God out, and your problems are all ended. If there is no God in heaven, then we have no problem about sin and suffering. . . . But the moment that you admit the existence of an all-powerful governing God, you are face to face with your problems. If you say that you have none, I question the strength of your faith.[1]

If there is a God, then what kind of a God is He?

Why isn't He big enough to do something about the "bad things" that happen to people, including His own people?

How big is God?

---

1. G. Campbell Morgan, *The Minor Prophets* (Old Tappan, NJ: Fleming H. Revell, 1960), 99.

How Big Is God?

The presence of suffering and moral evil in the world has given rise to a classic argument against the existence of God, or at least of a God who will do anything about them. Different people have expressed it in different ways, but it always contains the same elements. Here is the way the Greek philosopher Epicurus stated it:

> God either wishes to take away evil, and is unable; or He is able and unwilling; or He is neither willing nor able; or He is both willing and able.
>
> If He is willing but unable, He is feeble, which is not in accordance with the character of God. If He is able and unwilling, He is envious, which is equally at variance with God.
>
> If He is neither willing nor able, He is both envious and feeble, and therefore not God. If He is both willing and able, which alone is suitable for God, from what source then are evils? Or why does He not remove them?

When a sophomore philosophy student first encounters this argument, it appears to be very compelling. Reason would dictate that either there is no God, or that God is in some way limited and unable to do anything about the evils in the world.

There are at least two reasons why we must discuss the person and nature of God. As I mentioned in chapter 1, any solutions we come to for the problem of evil must be intellectually sound. We only complicate an already difficult problem if our reasoning is dishonest or immature. The second reason also relates to something I said in chapter 1: we live by promises, not by explanations. But these promises are only as good as the person who gives them. If God does not exist, then the promises are useless, and to believe them is to indulge in hopeless superstition. Or, if God exists but is unable to act, then His promises are vain. If God can't back up His promises with His power, then why trust Him? You are only endorsing checks drawn on a bankrupt account.

Some make a plea for a "limited God," arguing that God wants the best for us but cannot control the outcome of our lives. This suggests a God who is a concerned spectator but not an active participant.

We should not minimize the reality of evil. Those who tell us that evil is only "an illusion of the mind" are denying the concrete experiences of life. The same nervous system in my body that communicates pain also communicates to me the message that "pain is not real." Why should one message be "an illusion" but the other message real?

We should not try to solve the dilemma by saying that suffering is not important. It embarrasses me that some Christians take this approach and as a result alienate themselves (and the Christian message) from the very people who need them. To say that we should pay no attention to pain because one day we shall be in heaven is to misunderstand both pain and heaven. Whatever happens to God's people *now* is important both to them and to God, and we must not ignore it. This is not to say that our future hope plays no part in our dealing with suffering, because it does; but to try to *minimize* present suffering on the basis of future hope is to rob both of them of their power to build character and accomplish God's purposes in this world.

If, then, we don't eliminate or change suffering, we must be honest and either eliminate God or change our thinking about Him. We don't want to eliminate God because that creates a whole new set of problems, not the least of which is trying to explain both goodness and evil on the basis of evolution alone. But if we retain our belief in God, then what kind of a God are we to believe in? Logic would assume that we can believe only in a limited God who is unable to do very much about the problem of evil in the world.

The concept of a limited God is not new. The early Greek philosophers wrestled with the problems of change in the world. The basic idea is that everything in the world is a part of process, and this includes God. Philosopher Alfred North Whitehead was one of the thinkers who spearheaded this approach. "The process itself is the actuality" was his famous summary of this philosophy. God is part of the process. God is finite, not infinite, but He has the "potential for becoming infinite." You can still believe in God, but don't expect too much from Him.

It amazes me that people who have accepted this approach claim that it has "restored faith in God." I would like to remind them that *faith is only as good as the object of faith*. If the object of your faith is a limited God, what good is your faith? Instead of "restoring" your faith, this approach is *replacing* your faith with blind confidence in a theory.

I have serious problems with the idea of a limited God because this approach is contrary to reason and contrary to revelation.

Let's assume that God is a part of "process" and therefore is limited, but that He has the "potential" to become greater. How long has God been becoming? Six thousand years? A million years? How long will it take Him to get to the place where He can act? Is evil stronger than God? Are there two "Gods" in the universe, one good but feeble, the other evil but strong?

Wherever there is process, there is change. Can God change? *What* changes God? Whatever changes Him must be stronger than He is—and this means we have two Gods! Furthermore, anything involved in process can go backward as well as forward. What keeps God from regressing in character and power?

Some of these questions may seem to you as practical as "How many angels can dance on the head of a pin?" But I assure you, these questions are important. If God is limited and can't intervene in the affairs of the world or your life, then He is unable to judge evil. This means that morality is unimportant because God can never judge sin. A God who is too weak to deal with evil is too weak to judge it.

If God is a part of process, then we can never really know anything definite about Him because He is changing. This does away with the possibility of certain revelation from God and about God.

A limited God can do nothing about the future; for, after all, future events depend upon present decisions. If God is going to assure us some kind of hope for the future, He has to be doing something about it now. A God who cannot control the future or the present is not worth praying to, because He is helpless to intervene.

We end up asking the same question Thomas Hardy asked in his pessimistic (and agnostic) poem, "Nature's Questioning":

> We wonder, ever wonder, why we find us here!
> Has some Vast Imbecility,
> > Mighty to build and blend
> > But impotent to tend,
> Framed us in jest, and left us now to hazardry?

If we are going to "believe in" a limited God, then we must admit that we are giving a new meaning to the word "God." Because, by definition, God must be eternal, uncreated, perfect in love, power, and wisdom, and, because uncreated, unchanging and unchangeable. If we are to be honest in our thinking, we have no right to change the meaning of the word "God" *and then use it as though the meaning has not been changed.*

For example, how can I worship a limited God? All of the praise and worship that I find recorded in both the Old and New Testaments, and in hymnody, is centered on the greatness of God. It would appear to me that worship is out of the picture if God is not worthy of our praise.

Or take the matter of prayer. How can I pray to a God who permits my life to be the victim of "fate" or the plaything of "chance" or "luck"? Which of His many promises can I claim if He is unable to fulfill them?

Your personal character is also involved. Why bother to be good if everything (including God) is in process? Perhaps the traditional standards will change as the process continues. Even if you do "sin," it's unlikely that you will be judged. The evil force in the universe will not judge you because you are assisting it; and God apparently is unable to do much about evil.

In short, we are being intellectually and morally dishonest if we use the word "God" to mean a limited being who is not perfect. The "process" people (philosophers and theologians) have changed the meaning of "God" but they want us to go on using it in the traditional sense, and this is wrong.

Before we think about the matter of revelation, we need to deal with the Epicurean argument that opened this chapter. Is it as airtight as it appears? Not really, for the simple reason that the philosopher *already decided the question by the very way he presented it*. He started with the unproved presupposition that the only way God could exist would be in a universe that had no evil in it. What right did he have to make this assumption? "If there is evil in the world," he argued, "it is proof that God either does not exist or cannot do anything about it. But if He cannot do anything, then He is not God. Conclusion: God does not exist."

Actually, it is the very *presence* of evil in the world that assures us there is a God and that He is great enough to allow it to exist and still not be hindered in His working!

How big is God? He is far bigger than the limited mind of man can conceive! After I read the arguments of the philosophers and the "process" theologians, I want to ask them the question that God asked in Job 38:2, "Who is this that darkens my counsel with words without knowledge?"

God has revealed Himself to us in creation (including the personality of man), in history (His "mighty acts"), in the life and ministry of Jesus Christ, and in the Bible. All of these witnesses unite in declaring that God is great. "How great is God—beyond our understanding!" (Job 36:26). "For you are great and do marvelous deeds; you alone are God" (Ps. 86:10).

The prophet Isaiah certainly was captivated by the greatness of God.

> Do you not know?
>> Have you not heard?
> Has it not been told you from the beginning?
>> Have you not understood since the earth was
>>> founded?
> He sits enthroned above the circle of the earth,
>> and its people are like grasshoppers.
> He stretches out the heavens like a canopy,
>> and spreads them out like a tent to live in.
>
> "To whom will you compare me?
>> Or who is my equal?" says the Holy One.
> Lift your eyes and look to the heavens:
>> Who created all these?
> He who brings out the starry host one by one,
>> and calls them each by name.
> Because of his great power and mighty strength,
>> not one of them is missing.
>
> Do you not know?
>> Have you not heard?

The LORD is the everlasting God,
    the Creator of the ends of the earth.
He will not grow tired or weary,
    and his understanding no one can fathom.
He gives strength to the weary
    and increases the power of the weak.
Even youths grow tired and weary,
    and young men stumble and fall;
but those who hope in the LORD
    will renew their strength.
They will soar on wings like eagles;
    they will run and not grow weary,
    they will walk and not be faint. (Isa. 40:21–22, 25–
    26, 28–31)

Asaph, the psalmist, had this to say about the God he knew.

I will meditate on all your works
    and consider all your mighty deeds.
Your ways, O God, are holy.
    What god is so great as our God?
You are the God who performs miracles;
    you display your power among the peoples.
With your mighty arm you redeemed your people,
    the descendants of Jacob and Joseph.
The waters saw you, O God,
    the waters saw you and writhed;
    the very depths were convulsed. (Ps. 77:12–16)

Habakkuk is one of my favorite Old Testament prophets. If
ever a man of faith wrestled with the problem of God and evil,
it was Habakkuk; for he watched his own nation overwhelmed

by the idolatrous Babylonian forces. But his little book doesn't end with a funeral dirge; it ends with a song of praise! As he ponders the weakness of man, Habakkuk rejoices in the greatness of God.

> God came from Teman,
>> the Holy One from Mount Paran.
> His glory covered the heavens
>> and his praise filled the earth.
> His splendor was like the sunrise;
>> rays flashed from his hand,
>> where his power was hidden.
> Plague went before him;
>> pestilence followed his steps.
> He stood, and shook the earth;
>> he looked, and made the nations tremble.
> The ancient mountains crumbled
>> and the age-old hills collapsed.
> His ways are eternal. (Hab. 3:3–6)

How did the prophet respond to the devastating evil that the Babylonians brought with them? Did he abandon his faith in God or conclude that his God was too feeble to do anything? Quite the contrary! Habakkuk climaxed his little book with one of the greatest testimonies of faith found anywhere in religious literature.

> Though the fig tree does not bud
>> and there are no grapes on the vines,
> though the olive crop fails
>> and the fields produce no food,
> though there are no sheep in the pen
>> and no cattle in the stalls,

yet I will rejoice in the LORD,
I will be joyful in God my Savior.
The Sovereign LORD is my strength;
he makes my feet like the feet of a deer,
he enables me to go on the heights. (Hab. 3:17–19)

Try putting that testimony into contemporary terms!

Though the stock market crashes
and there is no money in the banks;
though the supply of fuel dwindles
and the machinery of society grinds to a halt;
though our ecological blunders ruin the crops
and there are barren shelves in the markets;
yet I will rejoice in the Lord,
I will be joyful in God my Savior!

After pondering God's ways in history, the apostle Paul sang a hymn of praise that extolled the greatness of God.

Oh, the depth of the riches of the wisdom and
knowledge of God!
How unsearchable his judgments,
and his paths beyond tracing out!
"Who has known the mind of the Lord?
Or who has been his counselor?"
"Who has ever given to God,
that God should repay him?"
For from him and through him and to him
are all things.
To him be the glory forever! Amen. (Rom. 11:33–36)

Can you imagine lifting that kind of praise to a God who is imperfect, limited, and in the process of trying to become infinite? Only an infinitely perfect God is worthy of our worship.

> You are worthy, our Lord and God,
>   to receive glory and honor and power,
> for you created all things,
>   and by your will they were created
>   and have their being. (Rev. 4:11)

If anybody had a right to question the power of God, it was the aged apostle John, exiled on the Isle of Patmos. He had been a faithful servant, and yet it appeared that the church was losing and the pagan Roman Empire was winning. Truth was not only "on the scaffold"; it appeared to be already dead and buried! Yet it was John who wrote down this hymn of praise:

> Great and marvelous are your deeds,
>   Lord God Almighty.
> Just and true are your ways,
>   King of the ages.
> Who will not fear you, O Lord,
>   and bring glory to your name?
> For you alone are holy.
> All nations will come
>   and worship before you,
> for your righteous acts have been revealed. (Rev. 15:3–4)

There is not one suggestion from any of these writers that God had been unfair or that life had robbed them of what they deserved. It was their suffering and their personal struggle against evil that brought strength to their hearts and praise to their lips! They were lost in the greatness of God.

What did they know that we today need to know? That God is greater than the evil in the universe and will one day triumph over it. They believed that the very presence of evil in the universe is a testimony to the greatness of God; for only a free and sovereign God can rule and overrule all of this evil and accomplish His eternal purposes. We may not understand all of His purposes and ways, but that isn't important. We know that He is working all things together for our good and His glory, and that is all that matters.

One task remains before we move on to the next chapter. If God is all-powerful (the theological term is *omnipotent*), why doesn't He exercise this power and deal with the evil in the world? If He indeed is sovereign, then He has the wisdom to know what to do and the power to be able to do it.

Again, we don't want to stumble into our "Epicurean fallacy" and make one issue a test of God's character. But something else is involved: many people don't really understand what is meant by the omnipotence (or sovereignty) of God. It is obvious that God cannot do anything that is contrary to His own nature or to the nature of the truth He has built into His universe. He cannot make a square circle; He cannot make a rock too heavy for Him to lift.

This does not mean that God is the victim of His own nature or is handicapped by the universe that He has created. Nor is He the victim of the freedom of choice that He has given to man. Among other things, God's omnipotence involves the fact that, in a world of natural law and human freedom (both ordained by God), He is able to accomplish His perfect will and yet remain true to His character and the principles He has built into His universe. The fact that God has imposed some limits on Himself (for instance, He will not manipulate people and violate their freedom of choice), in no way restricts His ability to accomplish His purposes.

God is greater than our problems. God is greater than our feelings. God is greater than the thoughts we have about Him or the words we use to talk about Him or even to praise Him. And it is His greatness that calls forth from us the kind of faith and courage that will keep us going when the going is tough.

> He heals the brokenhearted
> and binds up their wounds.
> He determines the number of the stars
> and calls them each by name. (Ps. 147:3–4)

Think of that! The God of the galaxies is the God who knows when your heart is broken—and He can heal it! He can number and name all the stars, and yet He watches over His people personally and individually! No wonder the psalmist went on to say:

> Great is our Lord and mighty in power;
> his understanding has no limit. (Ps. 147:5)

The greatness of God, however, is not a topic simply for philosophical or theological speculation. *If we believe it, we must do something about it.* Will we argue and try to limit God? Or will we believe and submit to God? Archbishop William Temple stated it correctly when he wrote, "The heart of Religion is not an opinion about God, such as philosophy might reach as the conclusion of its argument; it is a personal relation with God."

There are times when suffering strains that "personal relation," as in the case of Job. So we had better take time to get acquainted with Job and learn from his experiences.

Answers from an Ash Heap

While packing my library for our move from Chicago to Lincoln, Nebraska, I came across a box of term papers and other memorabilia from my seminary days. Here was a learned paper on the Book of Job! I winced as I read the following statement, written in my callow youth: "The fundamental theme of the Book of Job is suffering. It seeks to answer the age long question, 'Why do the righteous suffer?'"

It had been over thirty years since I had written those innocent words. Now, many years and tears later, I find I have to revise them. The basic theme of the Book of Job is *God*, not suffering, and the book answers very few questions. However, the Book of Job is an important document for our case that God is big enough to help us when life tumbles in.

The Old Testament is rich in its teaching about suffering. You don't find a complex "theology of suffering" so much as a sharing of the experiences of people who suffered and what they learned from it. Jacob suffered because he disobeyed God and made his way through life by second-guessing people and tripping them up. Joseph suffered because his brothers hated him, yet his suffering prepared him for his great opportunities in Egypt. Suffering is punishment, yet it can also be preparation.

The people of Israel suffered greatly, mainly because they disobeyed God's law and violated His covenant. But their suffering was also a revelation to the world that their God cared enough for them to deal with them when they strayed from the truth. Far from being a "mystery," suffering is often a blinding revelation of truth that we need to face up to honestly. To paraphrase Mark Twain, it's not what we *don't* know about God that should upset us, but what we *do* know. Calamity is often the voice of God shouting to us to turn around and come back.

But this was not the case with Job. He was a moral, religious man with a blameless reputation. God admitted that He had no reason to afflict Job (Job 2:3), and yet He put him through trials that would have broken a lesser man. The images Job used to picture his plight help us to sympathize with him.

> If I hold my head high, you stalk me like a lion
> and again display your . . . power against me. (10:16)

> The arrows of the Almighty are in me,
> my spirit drinks in their poison;
> God's terrors are marshaled against me. (6:4)

> Am I the sea, or the monster of the deep,
> that you put me under guard? (7:12)

> He has blocked my way so that I cannot pass;
> he has shrouded my paths in darkness. (19:8)

He tears me down on every side till I am gone;
    he uproots my hope like a tree. (19:10)

All was well with me, but he shattered me;
    he seized me by the neck and crushed me.
He has made me his target;
    his archers surround me. (16:12–13)

No wonder Job wanted to die! And no wonder his wife encouraged him to do so! He had lost his wealth and his children, and then his health had been taken from him. Job had faith in God, but when he turned to God for help, He was not there. The critical counsel of his friends was not what Job needed. "I desire to speak to the Almighty," he said, "and to argue my case with God" (13:3). He lifted his face to a silent heaven and cried, "Why do you hide your face and consider me your enemy?" (13:24).

If we ever hope to make any sense out of this ancient book, we must strip it down to its barest essentials: God, Satan, and Job. God and Satan were both interested in Job! God had proved His interest in Job by blessing him abundantly, and it was this blessing that attracted the interest of the Adversary.

Satan accused Job of being what the missionaries used to call a "rice Christian." Job served God only because God served Job. God provided abundant material blessings for Job, gave him a fine family (an important thing in the East), and then put a hedge about him so that all that he had was protected. "You claim that Job serves you because he loves you and trusts you," sneered Satan. "Have you ever dared to test him to see whether or not your evaluation is correct?"

Satan's accusation cuts at the very heart of worship and virtue. Is God worthy to be loved and obeyed even if He does not

41

bless us materially and protect us from pain? Can God win the heart of man totally apart from His gifts? In other words, the very *character of God* is at stake in this struggle!

But something else is also involved, and that's the character of virtue itself. Is all virtue really "enlightened selfishness"? Is it possible for us to serve God and our fellow humans from a heart of love, regardless of what we may "get out of it"? Satan would reply, "Absolutely not! True virtue is not possible because God is not worthy and man is not able."

Now we can understand why the Book of Job is a Jewish book, for only a believing Jewish writer would have bothered to wrestle with these problems. The Jewish faith declares that there is one God, and that He is good, just, and sovereign in all that He is and does. Furthermore, Judaism's statement of faith includes the fact that God is concerned about *individuals*. He is "the God of Abraham, and of Isaac, and of Jacob."

If the writer had believed in two "Gods," one good and the other evil, then his problem would have been solved. Or if he had believed in a limited God, instead of a sovereign God, he would have had no difficulties explaining Job's plight. As we have noted before, it is our *faith* that creates these problems for us; but it is also our faith that will help us to solve them.

In a very real sense, Job "helped God" to silence Satan and to settle it once and for all that God is worthy of our worship and service. Our faith and obedience must not be a "commercial" relationship between us and God. We must love the Giver and not just the gifts; for to love the gifts and not the Giver is the essence of idolatry.

How can we find out if our relationship to God is sincere or merely "commercial"? Well, how do *we* respond to God when we lose some of our blessings—our job, our investments, our loved ones, our health? This explains why Job had to endure such great losses; for until he was left with *nothing but God*, he would never have known what kind of faith he had. If only one or two of his children had perished, or a few dozen sheep, it would not have been a true test of his faith and love. He had to lose it all.

By the way, have you ever stopped to consider that Job paid a great price *for you and me*? Because he lost everything, and by his suffering proved Satan wrong, you and I don't have to lose everything. God can test us on a much smaller scale because the battle against Satan's lies has now been won by God.

It is worth noting that Job did not question the *fact* of his suffering but the *extent* of it. He didn't think himself to be above the difficult experiences of life; for, after all, he was a human being. But he was perplexed by the tremendous amount of suffering he had to endure. And, to add to his perplexity, he felt that God was far from him and that he was unable to communicate with Him. A strong "judicial image" runs through the Book of Job: God is the Judge, Job is the accused who is already enduring his sentence, but the accused has no way to present his case before the bench! "How then can I dispute with him?" Job asks. "How can I find words to argue with him?" (9:14). "But I desire to speak to the Almighty and to argue my case with God" (13:3). "Though I cry, 'I've been wronged!' I get no response; though I call for help, there is no justice" (19:7).

With this burden on his heart, Job cried out for a lawyer. "If only there were someone to arbitrate between us, to lay his hand upon us both" (9:33).

But it was of the utmost importance that Job *not* have the opportunity to argue his case before God, because that would have played right into the Adversary's hands. All Job had left was his faith in God, *and he was not sure where God was or what God was doing!* Had Job known the conflict taking place behind the scenes, it would have definitely affected his own responses. It was important that Job not know.

But we today *do* know! Thanks to Job's willingness to suffer and refute Satan's charges, we today can suffer by faith and know that God is working out His perfect purposes. Some suffering is the sad consequences of our disobedience. Some suffering is preparation for future ministry, as in the case of Joseph. But some suffering is simply for the glory of God, to refute Satan's charge that we obey God only to escape trials and enjoy blessings. There is often something bigger than ourselves involved in the trials that we are called to endure.

Robert Frost says perfectly in his poem "A Masque of Reason" when he has God say to Job:

> But it was of the essence of the trial
> You shouldn't understand it at the time.

It had to seem unmeaning to have meaning. Why? Because where there is "unmeaning" there must be faith. If we trust God, it must be because we know He is the kind of Person who can be trusted, *even though we may not always understand what He is doing.* The saintly Madame Guyon wrote, "In the commencement of the spiritual life, our hardest task is to bear with our neighbor; in its progress, with ourselves; and in its end, with God."

Now we can better understand the purpose that Job's friends fulfill in this drama. Without realizing it, they are Satan's helpers, his agents operating on earth. They have a "commercial" view of faith: if you obey God, he will bless you; if you disobey God,

He will punish you. On the basis of this dogma, they came to the conclusion that Job had to be a secret sinner or God would not have permitted him to suffer so much. Their repeated plea in their garrulous speeches is, "Job, get right with God! Confess your sins and he will restore your prosperity!"

But that is the very philosophy of hell! "Do what is right and you will escape pain and receive blessings." Is *that* why we obey God? Is virtue simply selfishness wearing a religious veneer? Or do we obey God because we love Him, regardless of how much pain He may permit in our lives?

You see, when a person practices "commercial faith," he has only two options when life tumbles in. He can bargain with God and get God to change the circumstances, or he can blame God for breaking the contract and thus refuse to have anything more to do with Him. Job's friends took the first approach and Job's wife took the second. His friends urged him to negotiate with God, confess his sins, and bargain his way back into blessing. His wife told him, "Curse God and die!" (2:9). Each of these options would fit perfectly into Satan's plan.

But Job rejected both options. Instead of cursing God, he blessed God: "The LORD gave and the LORD has taken away; may the name of the LORD be praised" (1:21). And instead of confessing his sins, Job maintained his integrity, and God commended him for this (2:3). "I will never admit you are in the right," Job told his accusing friends; "till I die, I will not deny my integrity" (27:5). Job was not claiming to be sinless, but he was refusing to be dishonest with himself, his friends, and his God, just so that he might escape suffering. He would not make bargains with God; for, if he did, he would be slandering the very character of God. And that is just what Satan

45

wanted him to do! Job was not simply defending Job; he was defending God.

Now that we better understand the setting and meaning of this complex book, we can focus on Job himself. Job did suffer; there is no question about that. He suffered when he lost his wealth, for, in the East, a man's position in society was determined for the most part by his possessions. Job had used his position to help others (see Job 29 for his testimony); now he was helpless himself. Job suffered even more when he lost his family; for bereavement is like amputation, and it never seems to heal. But as long as a man has his health, he can regain his wealth and start a new family; but then Job's health was taken from him. Except for Jesus Christ, perhaps no man named in the Bible suffered more than Job.

Keep this in mind when you read some of Job's pathetic outbursts. He cursed his birthday and wondered why he was born at all. He said some harsh things about his friends (although they may have deserved it), and he even hinted that God was carrying things a bit too far. In fact, Job even wanted to die and get it over with! Why? Because life seemed to have no purpose. "I despise my life," he said; "I would not live forever. Let me alone; my days have no meaning" (7:16).

But, after all, Job was simply being human; and nowhere did God condemn him for this. Job was hurting deeply and it was only normal for him to give expression to his feelings. It was his friends *who were trying to explain and defend God* who, in the end, were indicted by the Lord. "I am angry with you and your two friends," the Lord said to Eliphaz, "because you have not spoken of me what is right, as my servant Job has" (42:7). Job's words were honest and sincere, and they came from a broken heart.

Something else made a difference: Job was looking for a relationship with God, while his friends were looking for reasons to explain his plight. Job knew that God's people live by promises and not by explanations. Job was actually a threat to his friends. His experience challenged the validity of their cut-and-dried theology! "If Job is right with God," they were thinking, "then something is wrong with *our* faith." This meant that what happened to Job *could happen to them*! They were not really interested in Job as a hurting person. Their major interest was in Job as a problem to be removed, not as a person to be encouraged.

Job admitted that he was perplexed, but his friends were confident that they had all the right answers. "The fellowship of perplexity," writes Elton Trueblood, "is a goodly fellowship, far superior to the fellowship of easy answers."

The only thing that the New Testament has to say about Job is that he was a persevering man. "You have heard of Job's perseverance and have seen what the Lord finally brought about. The Lord is full of compassion and mercy" (James 5:11). One of the most difficult things in life is to wait *without a reason.* "Though he [God] slay me, yet will I hope in him" (Job 13:15). The Hebrew word translated "hope" means "to wait with confidence." Job persevered when there was every reason for him to quit. In fact, Job was confident that death itself would not prevent him from seeing God. "I know that my Redeemer lives," he affirmed, "and that in the end he will stand upon the earth. And after my skin has been destroyed, yet in my flesh I will see God; I myself will see him with my own eyes—I, and not another. How my heart yearns within me!" (19:25–27).

Job questioned God, and even accused God of being unjust, but he never lost his faith in God. In fact, Job's questions and accusations were in themselves evidences that he believed in a just and good God who would one day clear up all his problems and perplexities. His testimony of faith in 23:10 is one of the greatest found anywhere in religious literature: "But he knows the way that I take; when he has tested me, I will come forth as gold."

The apostle Peter had this same idea in mind when he wrote:

> In this you greatly rejoice, though now for a little while you may have had to suffer grief in all kinds of trials. These have come so that your faith—of greater worth than gold, which perishes even though refined by fire—may be proved genuine and may result in praise, glory and honor when Jesus Christ is revealed. (1 Pet. 1:6–7)

Patience and perseverance are important if our lives are to be successful. *The person who doesn't learn patience will have a difficult time learning anything else.* The only person who doesn't need patience is the one who can control all the people and circumstances in life—and no such person exists. If such a person did exist, he would be selfishness personified, because he would always have his own way. This is the philosophy of Satan.

Perhaps the most important thing we can say about Job's faith is this: he never questioned the sovereignty of God. The God he trusted was in charge of the universe (including Satan) and fully able to handle the situation. The Book of Job opens in the throne room of heaven, and as the story progresses, God never abandons that throne. The one name for God that is used more than any other in this book is "Almighty." You find this name forty-eight times in the entire Old Testament, and thirty-one of those instances are in Job.

At the beginning of his suffering, Job expressed confidence in the greatness of God. "His wisdom is profound, his power is vast," he said. "He alone stretches out the heavens and treads on the waves of the sea. . . . He performs wonders that cannot be fathomed, miracles that cannot be numbered" (9:4, 8, 10). At the close of his trial, Job still believed in the greatness of God: "I know that you can do all things; no plan of yours can be thwarted" (42:2).

Job would have had a difficult time believing that there are some things God does not or cannot control. After describing God's awesome power in nature, Job exclaimed: "And these are but the outer fringe of his works; how faint the whisper we hear of him! Who then can understand the thunder of his power?" (26:14).

Job would also have difficulty with those who call God unfair. Job realized that everything he had (and lost) came to him by the goodness and grace of God. "The LORD gave and the LORD has taken away; may the name of the LORD be praised" (1:21). He said to his wife, "Shall we accept good from God and not trouble?" (2:10).

In my pastoral ministry, I have heard people say in the midst of tragedy, "It's just not fair!" This is a normal response from a broken heart. But in the calm hour of reflection, we all realize that *fairness* is a dangerous philosophy of life. It can play right into the Satanic philosophy of serving God for what we can get out of it. "Lord, I'll play fair with you if you play fair with me." And there we are, bargaining again!

There were times when Job questioned God's justice. "Though I cry, 'I've been wronged!' I get no response; though I call for help, there is no justice" (19:7). In other words, the whole experience seemed one-sided: God could deal with Job, but Job had no access to God! "If it is a matter of strength," said the sufferer, "he is mighty! And if it is a matter of justice, who will summon him?" (9:19). Have you ever tried to subpoena God?

But Job learned that God makes no mistakes in the way He deals with His people. "Will the one who contends with the Almighty correct him?" the Lord asked Job. "Would you discredit my justice? Would you condemn me to justify yourself?" (40:2, 8). When I complain to God, "That isn't fair!" I am really saying, "God, I know more about this than You do!" But I don't!

Some years ago, one of our children complained to me about a decision her mother and I had made. "It isn't fair!" she said, and she backed up her words with her tears. My quiet response was, "Do you want your mother and me to manage our household only on the basis of what is fair?" She thought for a moment and replied, "No, I guess not." She remembered that the emphasis in our home was on love and grace, not on justice. If God did what was "fair," I wonder where any of us would be!

One of the reasons God did not answer Job's cries for justice was because He wanted to continue His relationship with Job on the basis of grace. God didn't want Job to have "commercial faith" based on a celestial contract. He wanted Job to have faith in a God with such richness of character—love, mercy, grace, goodness, kindness—that nothing could interfere with their relationship. The key question in the book of Job is not "Why do the righteous suffer?" but "Do we worship a God who is worthy of our suffering?" It's the courageous faith of Shadrach, Meshach, and Abednego when they had to choose between conformity and cremation:

> If we are thrown into the blazing furnace, the God we serve is able to save us from it, and he will rescue us from your hand, O king. But even if he does not, we want you to know, O king, that we will not serve your gods or worship the image of gold you have set up. (Dan. 3:17–18)

No "commercial faith" there! They worshiped a God worth dying for!

At the end of his time of trial, Job was healed and his family and fortune were restored. In fact, he had twice as much of everything! "The LORD blessed the latter part of Job's life more than the first" (42:12). These were blessings, not rewards. The Lord had given, the Lord had taken away, and the Lord had given again. It was pure grace from beginning to end.

Before we leave Job's ash heap, let's learn some practical lessons that can help us in the difficult times of life:

1. *Far more important than reasons and explanations is our personal relationship to God.* He loves us too much to harm us, no matter how much He may permit us to be hurt; and He is too wise to make a mistake. If you know God personally, through faith in Jesus Christ, then times of suffering can be times of deepening faith and of drawing closer to the Lord. No matter what Satan may say, God is worthy of our worship and service.

2. *God's purposes are often hidden from us.* He owes us no explanations. We owe Him our complete love and trust.

3. *We must be honest with ourselves and with God.* Tell God how you feel; He knows anyway, but it will do you good to be open and honest with Him. Maintaining a pious façade when you are hurting deeply only makes the hurt worse.

4. *Beware of cut-and-dried theologies that reduce the ways of God to a manageable formula that keeps life safe.* God often does the unexplainable just to keep us on our toes—and also on our knees. "For my thoughts are not your thoughts, neither are your ways my ways" (Isa. 55:8).

5. *Suffering is not always punishment for sin.* Sometimes it is, but not always. It doesn't hurt us to examine our own hearts, but we must not get carried away with the error of Job's three friends.

6. *In all of their suffering, God's people have access to God.* Job cried out for "an arbitrator" to bring him and God together, but that request was never granted. "If only there were someone to arbitrate between us, to lay his hand upon us both" (9:33). *There is such a Person!* He is Jesus Christ, the Savior, who today represents believers before the throne of God. "For there is one God and one mediator between God and men, the man Christ Jesus" (1 Tim. 2:5). Because Jesus Christ is both God and man, He is able to "lay his hand upon us both" and bring men and God together. He is a merciful and faithful High Priest on our behalf in heaven. Because of Christ, God's throne is not a throne of judgment; it is for His people a throne of grace.

In his delightful little book *Inward Ho!*, Christopher Morley writes: "I had a million questions to ask God: but when I met Him, they all fled my mind; and it didn't seem to matter."

There are over three hundred questions in the Book of Job, many of them asked by Job himself. But when Job met God, he said: "I am unworthy—how can I reply to you? I put my hand over my mouth. I spoke once, but I have no answer—twice, but I will say no more" (40:4–5). After hearing God speak about His greatness in creation, Job replied: "My ears had heard of you but now my eyes have seen you. Therefore I despise myself and repent in dust and ashes" (42:5–6).

When you and I hurt deeply, what we really need is not an explanation from God but a revelation of God. We need to see how great God is: we need to recover our lost perspective on life. Things get out of proportion when we are suffering, and it takes a vision of something bigger than ourselves to get life's dimensions adjusted again.

In the Bible, we have a revelation of God. We also have a revelation—a series of pictures—of what suffering means from the divine point of view. If we understand these "pictures of pain," it can help us better handle the difficulties of life.

Pictures of Pain

It has well been said that the mind of man is not a debating hall; it is a picture gallery. We may not realize it, but much of our thinking and feeling revolves around certain pictures, or metaphors, that seem to belong to the human race. These pictures show up repeatedly in our great art, music, and literature and help to form a common basis for looking at life.

For example, when Tennyson wrote his beautiful poem "Crossing the Bar," he was building on the metaphor of life as a voyage to a distant haven. Longfellow used the idea of sailing in his poem "The Building of the Ship," when he wrote:

> Thou, too, sail on, O Ship of State!
> Sail on, O Union, strong and great!

And Walt Whitman seems to have combined both ideas—the personal and the political—when he wrote concerning the death of Lincoln:

O Captain! my Captain! Our fearful trip is done,
The ship has weather'd every rack, the prize we sought
    is won.

Whenever anybody uses phrases like "He's drowning in debt," or "The whole thing is going to sink," he is comparing life to a voyage.

Some people see life as a battle, as warfare. Sometimes people greet us with, "Well, how goes the battle?" Hamlet compared life to a battle in his famous "To be, or not to be" soliloquy when he spoke about "the slings and arrows of outrageous fortune." In fact, he blended two metaphors—military and naval—when he considered taking up "arms against a sea of troubles."

Pregnancy and birth give us another series of metaphors. We sometimes speak of "giving birth to an idea," or perhaps we say that some project was "stillborn." Creative people often say they are "going through birth pangs" as they attempt to do their work.

Why do we use these and other metaphors as we discuss the important things of life? For one thing, these pictures help us get our hands on some complex experiences. It's much easier to talk about "the storms of life" than to go into the painful details. Even modern scientists are using metaphors (they call them "models") to help them understand and explain what's going on in the universe.

Also, these pictures involve our feelings as well as our minds. They prevent us from discussing the basics of life in a cold and detached way. Henry Wadsworth Longfellow could have said, "Trouble comes to everybody's life," and he would have been correct; but instead, he wrote:

> Be still, sad heart! and cease repining;
> Behind the clouds is the sun still shining;
> Thy fate is the common fate of all,
> Into each life some rain must fall,
>   Some days must be dark and dreary.

He used the image of the storm, not only to convey a truth to our minds, but also to get to our hearts.

Metaphors give us illumination—they help us *see* life—and also interpretation; they help us *understand* life. If life is a battle, then I had better learn how to fight! If it's a voyage, I had better learn how to swim! If Shakespeare is right and "All the world's a stage," then I had better read the script and find out the plot of the play before the curtain comes down!

I have said all this to introduce the subject of this chapter, namely, the metaphors for suffering and pain that are found in the Judeo-Christian tradition, as written in the Bible. No book is richer in this picturing of life than is the Bible. But these vivid metaphors are not there just as poetical decoration. They are important as God's revelation to us of what life, suffering, and death are all about. By the time we are through surveying some of the major metaphors, we will better understand, I think, why God permits His people to suffer.

The Book of Job is especially rich in metaphors. Except for the first two chapters and the last chapter, the Book of Job is a poem; and this itself is significant. Instead of giving us a series of lectures on suffering, the writer gives us a series of arresting pictures. Someone has called poetry "distilled emotion," and that is a good definition. It applies particularly to Job, because the dialogue in this book expresses the deep feelings of the participants, especially suffering Job.

It is interesting to discover the pictures Job gives of his own painful life. In chapter 7, he compares himself to a "hired man waiting eagerly for his wages" (vv. 1–5). "My days are swifter than a weaver's shuttle" (v. 6). His life is "but a breath" (v. 7). "As a cloud vanishes and is gone," so one day he will die and never be seen again (v. 9). In chapter 9, Job sees his days as "swifter than a runner" (v. 25). "They skim past like boats of papyrus, like eagles swooping down on their prey" (v. 26). Man's life is like a wilting flower and a fleeting shadow (14:2).

These images of the frailty and brevity of man's life have been used by writers over and over again, and will continue to be used. "All men are like grass," wrote Isaiah the prophet, "and all their glory is like the flowers of the field. The grass withers and the flowers fall, because the breath of the LORD blows on them. Surely the people are grass" (Isa. 40:6–7). Keep this image in mind the next time you read Walt Whitman's *Leaves of Grass*.

Now let's consider some of these images of suffering.

The Furnace

Often, when the Jewish nation was going through suffering, the experience was compared to being in a furnace. The familiar phrase "furnace of affliction" comes from Isaiah 48:10: "See, I have refined you, though not as silver; I have tested you in the furnace of affliction." The prophet was referring to the nation's captivity in Babylon; and the same image is found in Jeremiah 9:7 and Ezekiel 22:18–22.

But the furnace also reminded them of their years of suffering in Egypt. "But as for you," Moses told the people, "the LORD took you and brought you out of the iron-smelting furnace, out of Egypt, to be the people of his inheritance, as you now are" (Deut. 4:20).

Some of their prophets saw a future "furnace" experience for Israel, a time of intense tribulation. The prophet Zechariah wrote: "'In the whole land,' declares the LORD, 'two-thirds will be struck down and perish; yet one-third will be left in it. This third I will bring into the fire; I will refine them like silver and test them like gold'" (Zech. 13:8–9). You find the same image given in Malachi 3:2–3, a passage that Handel used in his oratorio "Messiah."

The metaphor of suffering as a furnace of fire carries with it a number of practical lessons. To begin with, there is always a purpose behind the suffering. The smith puts the ore into the furnace in order to purify it. From the molten metal, he removes the dross. With the metal, he manufactures a useful object. Times of suffering are times of testing: is our "ore" really worth anything? "For you, O God, tested us; you refined us like silver" (Ps. 66:10).

However, this refining process is not automatic. We who suffer must be willing to cooperate with God. God said to the prophet Jeremiah concerning the people of Jerusalem: "The bellows blow fiercely to burn away the lead with fire, but the refining goes on in vain; the wicked are not purged out. They are called rejected silver, because the LORD has rejected them" (Jer. 6:29–30).

Now we can better understand Job's famous statement: "But he [God] knows the way that I take; when he has tested me, I will come forth as gold" (Job 23:10). Job was willing to cooperate with God so that his experience of suffering might make him a better person. "The crucible for silver and the furnace for gold, but the LORD tests the heart" (Prov. 17:3).

What life does to us depends a great deal on what life finds in us. In my own pastoral ministry, I have seen some people bless God for their trials, and others curse God. When we have faith in God and depend on His grace, we can actually rejoice in times of suffering, even though we hurt. "In this you greatly rejoice," the apostle Peter wrote to some suffering Christians, "though now for a little while you may have had to suffer grief in all kinds of trials. These have come so that your faith—of greater worth than gold, which perishes even though refined by fire—may be proved genuine and may result in praise, glory and honor when Jesus Christ is revealed" (1 Pet. 1:6–7).

He also wrote: "Dear friends, do not be surprised at the painful trial you are suffering, as though something strange were happening to you. But rejoice that you participate in the sufferings of Christ, so that you may be overjoyed when his glory is revealed" (1 Pet. 4:12). "Painful trial" is literally "fiery trial."

The furnace of suffering has a way of testing the genuineness of our relationship with God. Is our faith real? Do we love Him for who He is or only for what He does for us? Are there areas in our lives that need to be cleansed? Are there areas that need to be strengthened and matured? The nation of Israel was forged and fashioned in the "furnace" of Egypt. When they disobeyed God, they were refined in the "furnace" of Babylonian captivity. Few nations in history have suffered as much as the Jews, and yet their suffering has helped to make them great.

If we trust God and depend on His grace, we can grow in personal character as we go through trials. "We also rejoice in our sufferings," wrote the apostle Paul, "because we know that suffering produces perseverance; perseverance, character; and character, hope" (Rom. 5:3–4). It is a remarkable thing that some of the most optimistic and enthusiastic people you will meet are those who have been through intense suffering.

The Storm

Longfellow was right: "Into each life some rain must fall." The image of the storm and the floods has been used almost universally to describe trials and sorrows. Of course, with the storm also comes *darkness*; and this, too, is a part of the image of suffering. "Deep calls to deep in the roar of your waterfalls," wrote David during a time of great danger and trial; "all your waves and breakers have swept over me" (Ps. 42:7). In another experience, he wrote: "Save me, O God, for the waters have come up to my neck. I sink in the miry depths, where there is no foothold. I have come into the deep waters; the floods engulf me" (Ps. 69:1–2).

"He would crush me with a storm," said Job (9:17). "He tears me down on every side till I am gone; he uproots my hope like a tree" (19:10). "God has made my heart faint; the Almighty has terrified me. Yet I am not silenced by the darkness, by the thick darkness that covers my face" (23:16–17). "You snatch me up and drive me before the wind; you toss me about in the storm" (30:22).

Storms are destructive. Tornadoes and hurricanes carry with them force that rivals that of bombs. Storms sometimes strike suddenly, when people have little time to make preparation. On the other hand, some storms can be predicted; but some people refuse to take the warnings seriously. But even if we can predict storms, we can't control them. The insurance policies call them "acts of God over which we have no control."

When I was a youngster, my family took an annual vacation in Door County, Wisconsin, where we would spend the week fishing. Since I have never been a good swimmer, I have never felt comfortable in a boat. One evening, we were out on the bay fishing, and we saw a storm coming across the water. My older brother started the motor on the boat, and we raced that storm across the bay! We arrived at the pier just in time to gather our equipment, cover our heads with the boat cushions, and run to the cottage, before the deluge hit.

But we don't always have the luxury of escaping the storm. Sometimes we have to experience it. Then what?

The image of the storm teaches us that God is ultimately in control of circumstances. There are some storms that we bring on ourselves. Jonah is a good example of this truth. "You hurled me into the deep," Jonah said to the Lord, "into the very heart of the seas, and the currents swirled about me; all your waves and breakers swept over me" (Jonah 2:3). It took a storm to bring Jonah to his senses and back into the place of obedience.

But there are some storms that God sends for our own good. "We went through fire and water," wrote the psalmist, "but you brought us to a place of abundance" (Ps. 66:12). When David looked back on a difficult and stormy period in his own life, he concluded, "I love you, O LORD, my strength. . . . As for God, his way is perfect. . . . The LORD lives! Praise be to my Rock! Exalted be God my Savior!" (Ps. 18:1, 30, 46). David was a better man after the storm.

We must keep in mind that God controls the storms: "lightning and hail, snow and clouds, stormy winds that do his bidding" (Ps. 148:8). He knows when we go into the storm, He watches over us in the storm, and He can bring us out of the storm when His purposes have been fulfilled. At the right time, He can say to the storm, "Hush, be still!" and make it a great calm (Mark 4:39). Meanwhile, He promises: "Fear not, for I have redeemed you; I have called you by my name; you are mine. When you pass through the waters, I will be with you; and when you pass through the rivers, they will not sweep over you" (Isa. 43:1–2).

God does not promise to keep us *out of* the storms and floods, but He does promise to sustain us *in* the storm, and then bring us out in due time for His glory when the storm has done its work.

Before we leave this metaphor, it is worth noting that God spoke to Job "out of the storm" (Job 38:1 and 40:6). Apparently, after Elihu's long speech, God darkened the heavens, aroused the wind, and brought a storm to the place where the men were conversing. *God does speak to us out of the storms of life.* Some of the greatest literature, art, and music, as well as humanitarian service, have come out of the storm experiences of life, when God spoke to one of His children. The important thing is that we trust Him and keep our ears tuned for His message.

Finally, our Lord Jesus used the image of baptism to describe His sufferings (Mark 10:38–40). He certainly could have said, "All your waves and breakers have swept over me!"

Warfare

"His anger burns against me," said Job; "he counts me among his enemies. His troops advance in force; they build a siege ramp against me and encamp around my tent" (Job 19:11–12). He pictures God as a deadly archer: "The arrows of the Almighty are in me, my spirit drinks in their poison" (6:4). "Why have you made me your target?" he asks God (7:20). "Again and again he bursts upon me," Job lamented; "he rushes at me like a warrior" (16:14). "Your forces come against me wave upon wave" (10:17).

The prophet Jeremiah used similar imagery when he described God's judgment on the city of Jerusalem when Babylon destroyed it. "Like an enemy he has strung his bow; his right hand is ready. Like a foe he has slain all who were pleasing to the eye. . . . The Lord is like an enemy; he has swallowed up Israel" (Lam. 2:4–5).

The apostle Paul often used military images in his writing. "Endure hardship with us like a good soldier of Christ Jesus," he wrote to young Timothy (2 Tim. 2:3). He also admonished his young understudy to "fight the good fight" (1 Tim. 1:18). If God's people are going to win the battle of life, they must use by faith the equipment God has provided for them. This equipment is explained in Ephesians 6:10–18.

There are difficult times in our lives when Jeremiah's lament seems to be true: "The Lord is like an enemy" (Lam. 2:5). Sometimes, by our disobedience, *we* are the ones who have declared war on God! "Anyone who chooses to be a friend of the world becomes an enemy of God" (James 4:4). But sometimes God permits battles to come our way in order to discipline us and equip us for more effective service. Paul was in a "military mood" when he wrote: "Be on your guard; stand firm in the faith; be men of courage; be strong" (1 Cor. 16:13).

God never promised to pamper and shelter His people. He did promise to strengthen us for the battle and help us to win the victory. "Do not pray for easy lives," said Phillips Brooks.

"Pray to be stronger men. Do not pray for tasks equal to your powers. Pray for powers equal to your tasks." The apostle John echoed that admonition when he wrote, "This is the victory that has overcome the world, even our faith" (1 John 5:4).

The Harvest

A number of agricultural images cluster about the theme of suffering. "Threshing" is often used as a picture of judgment. "His winnowing fork is in his hand," warned John the Baptist, "and he will clear his threshing floor, gathering the wheat into his barn, and burning up the chaff with unquenchable fire" (Matt. 3:12).

The difficulties of life are also like a sifting process, as when the farmer separates the wheat from the chaff. Jesus told Peter, "Simon, Simon, Satan has asked to sift you [all of the disciples] as wheat. But I have prayed for you, Simon, that your faith may not fail" (Luke 22:31). The prophet Amos used this same image in describing the trials Israel would face in the world (Amos 9:9).

Of course, one of the obvious lessons from this agricultural metaphor is that we reap what we sow. Eliphaz reminded Job of this fundamental principle of life: "As I have observed, those who plow evil and those who sow trouble reap it" (Job 4:8). "Do not be deceived: God cannot be mocked. A man reaps what he sows. The one who sows to please his sinful nature, from that nature will reap destruction; the one who sows to please the Spirit, from the Spirit will reap eternal life" (Gal. 6:7–8).

We not only reap *what* we sow, but we also reap *in propor-tion* as we sow. "Remember this: Whoever sows sparingly will also reap sparingly, and whoever sows generously will also reap generously" (2 Cor. 9:6). However, the harvest may not come immediately, or even during our lifetime. But the Lord will see to it that the good seeds we have sown will produce fruit.

Jesus used the image of the seed to illustrate what it means to live your life for the glory of God. Let me quote the entire passage because it is an important one for our study.

> Jesus replied, "The hour has come for the Son of Man to be glorified. I tell you the truth, unless a kernel of wheat falls to the ground and dies, it remains only a single seed. But if it dies, it produces many seeds. The man who loves his life will lose it, while the man who hates his life in this world will keep it for eternal life. Whoever serves me must follow me; and where I am, my servant also will be. My Father will honor the one who serves me. Now my heart is troubled, and what shall I say? 'Father, save me from this hour'? No, it was for this very reason I came to this hour. Father, glorify your name!" (John 12:23–28)

Of itself, a seed is not a beautiful thing; and certainly being buried in the ground is not an inviting prospect. *But the future results compensate for these difficulties.* The seed accepts the present because it lives for the future—beauty and fruitfulness. Our Lord's suffering and death were not "beautiful experiences" by any means, yet they led to glory, not only for God, but for all who will trust Him.

"Why have you buried yourself in this forsaken place?" a man asked a foreign missionary.

"I haven't buried myself," the missionary replied. *"I was planted."*

That makes all the difference! If our suffering is a part of God's "planting," then we can accept it by faith and know that

He will bring out of our experiences that which will help others (beauty and fruitfulness) and glorify His name. If you are living by faith, you are never "buried"; you are planted. You don't pray, "Father, save me!" but instead you pray, "Father, glorify your name" (John 12:27, 28). If we save our lives for ourselves, we will lose them; if we yield our lives, we will save them and multiply them.

Another repeated agricultural image in the Bible is that of the vineyard. In John 15, Jesus compared His relationship with His followers with that of the vine to the branches: we must abide in Him and draw from Him the spiritual power we need for life and service. Only then can we be fruitful and feed others. Jesus said that His Father was the gardener who cared for the branches, and one of the duties of the vinedresser is to trim the branches. *It is the fruitful branches that He prunes.* Jesus said, "Every branch that does bear fruit he trims clean so that it will be even more fruitful" (John 15:2).

If the branches could speak, I'm sure they would complain when they are pruned. But apart from the pruning, there could be no fruitfulness. Sometimes our suffering is a pruning process. As with the vinedresser, God removes not the bad things, but the good things that are keeping us from the better and the best. The vinedresser cuts away excess wood and leaves so that the vine may produce choice fruit. Suffering is not always punishment for sin, in spite of what Job's friends may say. Sometimes our suffering is a pruning experience, during which God carefully removes *good* things so that we may become more useful to Him and to others.

And even after the ripe grapes are produced, there is still another process: the winepress. In the Bible, this is often used as a picture of judgment. In the destruction of Jerusalem, Jeremiah saw the Lord crushing His people in the winepress (Lam. 1:15). In God's judgment of the nations at the end of the age, Isaiah has the Lord saying, "I have trodden the winepress alone. . . . I trampled them in my anger and trod them down in my wrath" (Isa. 63:3). The apostle John picked up this image in his description of Armageddon in Revelation 14:14–20.

Associated with the winepress is the image of the cup. Isaiah saw the Babylonian captivity as Israel drinking a cup of wrath from the hand of God (Isa. 51:17–22), and Jeremiah repeated the image (Jer. 25:15–29). But Jesus used the drinking of the cup as the image of *surrendering to the will of God*. When Peter drew a sword and tried to defend Jesus in the garden, the Lord said, "Put your sword away! Shall I not drink the cup the Father has given me?" (John 18:11). The contrast between the sword and the cup is interesting: *fighting* the will of God or *accepting* the will of God. Can we be afraid of a cup that the Father mixes for us and gives to us in love?

How strange it is that people should accept the laws of nature, such as sowing, reaping, or pruning, and learn to cooperate with them, and yet reject these same principles when they are applied to the spiritual life. If I enjoy my breakfast juice, cereal, toast, it's because some seeds died and produced a harvest. Should I be so selfish that I refuse to permit God to "plant" me, grind me in the mill, or crush me in the press, so that my life might feed others?

Before we leave the agricultural images, we should make note of the word *tribulation*, which in the English language comes from the Latin word *tribulum*. A tribulum was a heavy wooden frame with iron spikes beneath it. This frame was drawn by oxen across the threshing floor so that the grain was separated from the chaff. (The Latin word *tribulare* means "to rub out corn, hence to afflict.") So, the next time you talk about your "tribulations," keep this image in mind.

Travail and Birth

"I hear a cry as of a woman in labor," wrote Jeremiah, "a groan as of one bearing her first child" (Jer. 4:31). The prophet saw the impending invasion by Babylon as a "travail experience" for his people. Jesus used the same image when He described the future tribulation that will come upon the earth: "All these are the beginning of birth pains" (Matt. 24:8). The apostle Paul amplified this statement: "While people are saying, 'Peace and safety,' destruction will come on them suddenly, as labor pains on a pregnant woman, and they will not escape" (1 Thess. 5:3).

It is interesting the way Jesus applied this image to His own suffering, death, and resurrection. He comforted His disciples by saying: "I tell you the truth, you will weep and mourn while the world rejoices. You will grieve, but your grief will turn to joy. A woman giving birth to a child has pain because her time has come; but when her baby is born she forgets the anguish because of her joy that a child is born into the world. So with you: Now is your time of grief, but I will see you again and you will rejoice, and no one will take away your joy" (John 16:20–22).

Travail is painful, but it is also purposeful; and it is the achieving of this happy purpose that makes the travail meaningful and worthwhile. *The same baby that helps to cause the pain also brings the joy!* Christ gives us joy, not by substitution, but by *transformation*. He does not always take the pain away, but

He uses the pain to give birth to joy. We are not saved *from* our travail; we are saved *by* our travail.

I have yet to pick up a hymnal that does not contain at least one song written by Fanny J. Crosby. Because of the stupidity of a doctor, she was blinded at the age of six weeks. As she grew older, she saw in this "accident" the providential hand of God. She wrote her first poem at the age of eight. Here it is:

> O what a happy soul am I!
>   Although I cannot see,
> I am resolved that in this world
>   Contented I will be,
> How many blessings I enjoy
>   That other people don't!
> So weep and sigh because I'm blind,
>   I cannot, and I won't.

Her travail gave birth to a gift of song, a gift that has enriched millions of worshipers in churches around the world. Because of her faith in Christ, a so-called handicap became a tool that she used to bring joy and encouragement to many.

Paul used the image of travail to describe the present condition of creation. "We know that the whole creation has been groaning as in the pains of childbirth right up to the present time" (Rom. 8:22). God made it a *good* creation: "God saw all that he had made, and it was very good" (Gen. 1:31). But today, it is a *groaning* creation because of the effects of man's disobedience to God. However, one day it shall be a *glorious* creation when "creation itself will be liberated from its bondage to decay and brought into the glorious freedom of the children of God" (Rom. 8:21).

People sometimes ask, "How can a loving God cause sickness, storms, and other disasters that cause so much damage and heartache?" They forget that the world we know is not the world God originally created. It was *man's* disobedience that plunged creation into the bondage of sin and death. But even this bondage is marked by travail: one day there will be "a new birth of freedom." Paul was not discouraged by personal trials or natural disasters—and he had experienced a good deal of both! "I consider that our present sufferings are not worth comparing with the glory that will be revealed in us. The creation waits in eager expectation for the sons of God to be revealed" (Rom. 8:18–19).

Just as there can be no birth without travail, there can be no glory without suffering. The seed is willing to "suffer" in anticipation of future glory. The mother is willing to suffer in anticipation of the joy of holding her beloved baby.

This principle is illustrated in a poignant episode in the life of Jacob. Here is the account:

> Then they moved on from Bethel. While they were still some distance from Ephrath [Bethlehem], Rachel began to give birth and had great difficulty. And as she was having great difficulty in childbirth, the midwife said to her, "Don't be afraid, for you have another son." As she breathed her last—for she was dying— she named her son Ben-Oni [son of my trouble]. But his father named him Benjamin [son of my right hand]. (Gen. 35:16–18)

Imagine going through life with a name like "Son of my trouble." Every time somebody addressed you, he would be reminding you that your birth helped to take your mother's life! By faith, Jacob renamed the baby "Benjamin." He gave him a name that carried dignity and triumph. In our experiences of travail, we need to trust God and dare to believe that the results will be triumph and not sorrow, no matter how much we may hurt. The tribe of Benjamin became a noble people in Israel and gave the nation her first king. They also gave the world the apostle Paul.

Running the Race

Statements like "he has run the race" or "she has finished her course" often appear as epitaphs, because we picture a man's life as a race: it has a beginning, a course, an ending, and (we trust) a reward. It takes discipline and dedication to stay on course and finish the race successfully, in spite of the obstacles in the way.

The Greeks and Romans were big on sports, so this image is often found in the New Testament; but there are a few Old Testament references. Perhaps the most famous is Ecclesiastes 9:11: "I have seen something else under the sun: The race is not to the swift or the battle to the strong." To Solomon, life was a race through a battlefield! The point he was making was simply that nobody should depend *only* on his natural abilities; they are no guarantee of success.

One of my favorite "running" texts is Jeremiah 12:5: "If you have raced with men on foot and they have worn you out," God said to his discouraged prophet, "how can you compete with horses? If you stumble in safe country, how will you manage in the thickets by the Jordan?" In other words, "If you think the going is tough now, Jeremiah, just wait! The race will get harder! But this is the only way I can prepare you for what lies ahead."

Each new demand of life helps us to grow. We are not really competing with footmen and horses; *we are competing with ourselves.* In a television interview, an Olympic winner was asked, "Were you watching the competition?" He replied, "I never watch the competition. I watch the clock. I'm competing with myself, not with them."

The prophet Isaiah has a great promise for us as we seek to run the race of life: "But those who hope in the LORD will renew their strength. They will soar on wings like eagles; they will run and not grow weary, they will walk and not faint" (Isa. 40:31).

The New Testament often uses the race as a picture of life and service. John the Baptist "fulfilled his course" (Acts 13:25 KJV), and he did so courageously. This was Paul's great desire: "However, I consider my life worth nothing to me, if only I may finish the race and complete the task the Lord Jesus has given me" (Acts 20:24). At the end of his life he wrote: "I have fought the good fight, I have finished the race, I have kept the faith" (2 Tim. 4:7). He looked upon his life as an appointed race with an anticipated reward (Phil. 3:12–14).

But the race is not easy! This is the theme of Hebrews 12, written to some of God's people who were going through suffering. In the previous chapter, the writer points out that *all* of God's people suffered in one way or another, yet their faith brought them through to victory. The greatest example is Jesus Christ, who "endured the cross" and today is seated in glory. Because of His victory, He can help us win the race and gain the prize. In the light of these many victories of faith, "let us run with perseverance the race marked out for us" (12:1).

One of the key words in Hebrews 12 is *discipline*, which basically means "child-training." Greek and Roman boys were expected to enroll in the local gymnasia and participate in the athletic contests. It was a part of their training for manhood. If life is a race, an athletic contest, then we must discipline ourselves if we hope to be winners. "Endure hardship as discipline; God is treating you as sons" (Heb. 12:7). In other words, "If you want to mature, expect some trials. They are a part of the race of life."

In spite of the fact that my two brothers have always been interested in sports, and my four children are all athletically inclined, I am not an athlete. Golf seems to me to be a great way to ruin a good walk. Competitive sports take time away from things I enjoy doing much more. But I do know this much about athletics: If you play the game right, you will benefit from the experience. Far more important than winning is being the kind of person who *can* win.

"No discipline seems pleasant at the time, but painful. Later on, however, it produces a harvest of righteousness and peace for those who have been trained by it" (Heb. 12:11).

The trials I experience in the race of life may not seem good to me now, but God promises that they will benefit me later on. I must not be content to run with the footmen; I must compete with the horses if I ever expect to develop myself. It's easy to run in the safe country, but I won't mature unless I tackle the Jordan jungles. If I am going to grow, I must be challenged.

Trial

The judicial image is very strong in the Book of Job. The suffering patriarch saw himself as a helpless victim, arrested by God, convicted, and not given any opportunity for appeal. "Even if I summoned him and he responded," Job complained, "I do not believe he would give me a hearing" (9:16). "Since I am already found guilty, why should I struggle in vain?" (9:29). "But I desire to speak to the Almighty and to argue my case with God" (13:3).

We have already considered this aspect of suffering when we surveyed the Book of Job. But there are some lessons associated with this judicial picture that we need to discuss briefly.

Like Job's "comforters," when tragedy strikes, we immediately think of guilt. Who is to blame? Even our Lord's disciples were not immune to this kind of thinking. "Rabbi, who sinned, this man or his parents, that he was born blind?" (John 9:2). As a pastor, I have often had to counsel with people whose only approach to suffering was to feel guilty and throw themselves on the mercy of the court. In some cases, this was the right approach, because they *had* deliberately disobeyed God and were suffering the consequences. But it is not appropriate in every case.

God does enforce the laws that He has put into this universe. But each law is a two-edged sword: if we cooperate with it, it will work for us; if we violate it, it will work against us. Fire can produce warmth and power; it can also produce burns and destruction! The proper dose of medicine can assist healing; too large a dose can kill the patient. The same God determined both results; and if we want to enjoy the benefits, we must respect the dangers. God has given us minds and He expects us to use them.

There is a sense in which our times of suffering are also times of trial, even if we are not guilty of disobeying God. We are "on trial," as it were, to prove that our faith in Christ is genuine. God has every right to try us so that *we* might learn more about ourselves and our relationship with God. It was in this sense that God tested Abraham when He asked him to sacrifice Isaac on the altar (Genesis 22).

However, when God's children are "called into court," we must remember that *our Father is the Judge.* "As a father has compassion on his children, so the LORD has compassion on those who fear him" (Ps. 103:13). This does not mean that God winks at sin or pampers rebellious children. But it does mean that He is not dealing with us on the basis of law alone, but also on the basis of grace.

"The LORD is compassionate and gracious, slow to anger, abounding in love. He will not always accuse, nor will he harbor his anger forever; he does not treat us as our sins deserve or repay us according to our iniquities" (Ps. 103:8–10).

"Our fathers disciplined us for a little while as they thought best; but God disciplines us for our good, that we may share in his holiness" (Heb. 12:10).

In other words, the trial is not for the purpose of condemnation, but for our personal good. God does not want to imprison us; He wants to set us free—provided that we have learned how to use our freedom in a mature way.

These, then, are some of the major "pictures of pain" found in the Bible. There are some minor images, but they need not be considered now. All that remains is for us to gather up some of the practical lessons that these pictures teach us, lessons that can help us when we are suffering.

1. *God has not promised to make us comfortable, but He has determined to make us conformable.* He will put us into the furnace to remove the dross and to make us moldable in His hands. But keep this in mind: when you are in the furnace,

your Father keeps His eye on the clock and His hand on the thermostat. He knows just how much we can take.

2. *The battles of life are not easy, but God has given us the equipment we need to succeed.* Each victory prepares us for the next assault. The race of life is not easy, but as we accept each new challenge, we grow and can accomplish more.

3. *We need patience.* The harvest doesn't come immediately. God doesn't bury us; He plants us. And He promises that our experience will produce a harvest.

4. *Times of travail can be times of birth.* Today's suffering can mean tomorrow's glory. God is not accomplishing all His purposes today, nor is He explaining all His plans. We do not need to give birth to a Ben-Oni; we can give birth to a Benjamin.

5. *The storms are frightening, but God can speak to us out of the whirlwind.* Even the storms can fulfill His will.

6. *Yield to the pruning knife; it will make us more fruitful.* Accept the cup that the Father gives us.

I have referred often in this chapter to the Babylonian captivity of the Jews, one of the most humiliating and trying experiences this noble nation has ever had. After the captivity had begun, the prophet Jeremiah sent the exiles a letter of encouragement; and in that letter is this promise from the Lord:

> "For I know the plans I have for you," declares the LORD, "plans to prosper you and not to harm you, plans to give you hope and a future." (Jer. 29:11)

The next time you are in the storm, or the battle, or you feel you are on trial, or going through travail, or suffering in the furnace, meditate on that promise. Here is what it says: God is thinking about you personally, and is planning for you in ways that you could never understand, let alone imagine. Let Him have His way. Your future is secure if you are trusting Him.

If you wallow in self-pity, then the pictures of pain will become mirrors, and all you will see is yourself.

But if you trust Jesus Christ and commit yourself to Him, the pictures will become windows through which you will see God and the vast horizons of blessing He is preparing for you.

Which will it be? Mirrors—or windows?

The God Who Cares

've found the Bible verse that describes my life perfectly," a distraught man informed me in a counseling session. He picked up my Bible from the desk and opened it to Job 5:7.

"Here—read that!"

I read the verse aloud: "Yet man is born to trouble as surely as sparks fly upward."

"I was *born* to trouble," he lamented, "I *live* in trouble, and I'll probably *die* in trouble! There's always a new bunch of sparks, and they're burning me something awful!"

It had to be a flash of divine guidance, because I handed the Bible back to him and said, "There's another verse that goes along with Job 5:7. It's 1 Peter 5:7—read it!"

He read: "Cast all your anxiety on him because he cares for you."

He was silent for a time, and then he said, without even looking up, "Yeah, but how do I know that God *really* cares for me?"

If we could be sure that there is a caring God watching over us, concerned about our pain and our problems, all of us would have a much easier time coping with life. But sometimes the very problems we encounter and the pains we endure seem to contradict 1 Peter 5:7. In our moments of reluctant honesty we find ourselves agreeing with Gideon when he asked the angel of the Lord, "But sir, if the LORD is with us, why has all this happened to us?" (Judg. 6:13).

Of course, it would be easy to quote some of the great promises from the Bible, proving that God cares; but there are times when even those familiar promises seem to mock us. I'm not going to ignore those promises; but before we get to them, there are some other matters that must be tended to first.

If you were God, how would you go about convincing people that you really cared *about* them and *for* them?

Over the years, I've received different answers to that important question. One of the most frequent is, "I would have made a better world to begin with!" This means, of course, a world without evil and without pain.

Let's think about that answer. Why didn't God make a "better world" in the first place? While God is not the author of evil, He permitted evil to appear on the scene, and He has not yet eliminated it from His world. Surely He could have done a better job! At some point, they suggest, He should have said, "Back to the drawing board!"

The first thing you must realize is that we are dealing with a hypothetical question, and hypothetical questions are not easy to answer *if* they can be answered at all. Nobody can prove that any other world would necessarily be a better world. In fact, each of us brings to this question a preconceived idea of what "better" is all about. What may be a "better world" for an Adolf Hitler would most certainly be a "worse world" for most other people. If you have ever tried to plan a vacation for four children, you have some idea of what it means to try to please everybody!

But something else is true: The standards and values that we have in mind for this "better world" actually came *from the world we live in right now.* We did not get these "better ideas" by visiting another planet or receiving a communication from outer space. This means, of course, that we are being inconsistent; we take our standards from *this* world, yet we say we want a *better* world. We are admitting that God *has* put some good things into this world after all!

It does us little good, I think, to speculate about the world God *might have created.* When we hurt, we have to deal with realities. However, when we deal with these realities, we must try our best to be honest and factual. Most of us have a tendency to let our imaginations take over in times of crisis or tragedy.

Perhaps the most difficult situations a pastor must deal with are the death of a child and the suicide of a young person. All ministries to the bereaved are difficult, but these two situations seem to demand the most. Why does an innocent child die? Why would a promising youth take his or her own life? "What this baby might have become!" sighs some relative at the funeral. But, quite frankly, *nobody knows what the baby might have become.* He might have become a great inventor—or a hardened criminal. We don't know; and, because we don't know, we are wise not to speculate. Lasting comfort cannot be based on suppositions.

What is true of the baby's death and the youth's suicide is true of the world; we only make matters worse by speculating. Since this *is* the world that God made, I have to believe that He knew what He was doing. "Whom did the Lord consult to enlighten him," asked Isaiah, "and who taught him the right way?" (Isa. 40:14). Speculating about a hypothetical "better world" may inflate my ego, but it can never solve my problems or help me to handle my suffering creatively.

Other people believe that, though God is not responsible for evil in the world, He could do more about eliminating it. "If I were God," is their reply, "I would let people know I really cared by intervening and eliminating from the world everything that is evil and that causes suffering."

Now, nobody is opposed to the high ideals set by this reply. I remember how happy my wife and I were when the Salk vaccine was developed and we could protect our children against polio. All of us would give thanks to God if somebody came up with a cure for cancer or diabetes. As God's people, we don't calmly accept the status quo with a pious, "God wills it." The fact that Jesus healed people when He ministered on earth is argument enough for us to do all we can to promote wholeness in man.

But the suggestion that God intervene and "clean house" presents us with some practical difficulties. To begin with, it really isn't a new suggestion at all; it puts us right back on square one. Each of us has his own idea of "a better world," and, as I mentioned before, we get our ideas from the world we're now living in, a world created and controlled by God. Whether God makes the world from the beginning as we want it, or whether He intervenes and straightens things out, is really about the same thing.

But there is a second consideration: What do these people mean by "God intervening" in the affairs of the world? Are they suggesting that God today is *outside His world*? If there is one lesson Jesus tried to get across in His teaching it was *the presence of the Father in the world*. The Father gives the lilies their glory, and He is there when the sparrow drops dead. He is not an absentee King; He is an ever-present Friend.

We must be very careful here, because *God is not the world*. That's pantheism and it's a false definition of God's relationship to creation. Nor is God "being made" by the world, as a part of the creative process. That's our old enemy "process theology" again, and it is wrong. Both the Old Testament and the New Testament make it clear that God is the Creator, and therefore is apart from the world, above it, and transcendent; but He is also present in the world, working out His purposes, and therefore immanent.

"Heaven is my throne and the earth is my footstool," God said through the prophet Isaiah. "Has not my hand made all these things, and so they came into being? . . . This is the one I esteem: he who is humble and contrite in spirit, and trembles at my word" (Isa. 66:1–2). The God who dwells in heaven is willing to dwell also in the heart of the humble believer! He is both above us and within us, transcendent and immanent, to use theological terms.

If, then, we ask God to "intervene," we are suggesting that He is absent. We are also suggesting that things are happening that may take Him by surprise, so that He must suddenly act or His entire plan will go down the drain. We are describing a "superman" kind of God, the Greek and Roman *deus ex machina*, the god who swoops down at just the right time and quickly solves the problem. But the God I worship doesn't have to be brought on stage to solve problems. *He wrote the script!* For that matter, He is in charge of the drama, and He will see to it that everything works out right because He is also one of the actors in the play.

The suggestion that God intervene and make everything good presents another problem: *How* do you make things good? Can you *force* goodness? Can God *force* a man to love his wife and abandon his mistress? Is God free to violate the very freedom that He gave to man, a freedom that is a part of the image of God in man?

Granted, it would be relatively simple for God to change material things as opposed to moral creatures. Everything in nature obeys the Creator, as Jesus demonstrated when He was ministering on earth. God can speak to cancer cells and remove them. God can heal sick and broken bodies; I have seen Him do it and I have experienced it in my own life. A drunken driver hit my car going ninety miles an hour; and when I arrived at the hospital, the chaplain told my wife, "He'll never make it through the night." But our church family gathered to pray, and in two weeks, I was home.

It is one thing for God to change *things*; it is quite another for Him to change *people*. And much of the evil in this world is caused by people, not by things. Even if God did remove all the diseases that plague us today, and all the things that cause pain, we would not necessarily have a better world. We would only have the same old people living in a more comfortable world—and the absence of pain might make it easier to sin!

When discussing these matters, I sometimes shock people by asking them, "*Why* do you want to see the world changed and all the bad things eliminated?" Their usual answer is, "So that we can enjoy life more." Then I ask, "Do you think you would be a *better person* if you enjoyed life more?" Too often, that question goes unanswered.

The purpose of life is not enjoyment, to the exclusion of building character and glorifying God. We have no guarantee that a better environment would produce better people, that the absence of disease and pain would also mean the absence of hatred and deceit. How many times I've heard in the intensive care ward, "Pastor, if the Lord brings me through this, I'll be the best person you've ever seen." In some cases, the Lord did bring them through; but they didn't always prove to be better people.

I have a feeling that the "bad things" that stalk our lives are accomplishing purposes we may not fully understand today. Only a great and sovereign God could (humanly speaking) "take the risk" to permit evil in His world, and still work out His perfect plan. We can't explain each individual case, but the total pattern seems to be clear: God is in control and is working out His purposes for our good and His glory. As the old Puritan, Thomas Watson, used to say, "Where reason cannot wade, there faith must swim."

We are back to our original question: If you were God, how would you convince people that you really cared for them? Would you do it any differently than the way you *now* show concern to the people you know and love?

Since we are made in the image of God, our care for others is probably some kind of reflection of His care for us. As parents and grandparents, we express our care by providing for needs, speaking words of love and encouragement, teaching, warning, helping to share burdens, and occasionally digging down and paying bills. We try to avoid pampering and overprotecting our children and grandchildren, because we know they have to accept challenges if they are to mature successfully.

Imagine a child saying to his parents, "I keep skinning my knees on the sidewalk! If you really loved me, you'd get that mean sidewalk out of here!" We don't remove the sidewalk; we help to teach the child how to walk, roller skate, or ride the bike with skill and caution. Crossing a busy street is a dangerous enterprise, but we don't help the child by eliminating the vehicles. Instead, we put up traffic lights, teach the child to look both ways, and warn him that the consequences of carelessness are painful.

God shows that He cares for us by providing for us. He has given us a world that is filled with everything we need for life and health. "He has shown kindness by giving you rain from heaven and crops in their seasons; he provides you with plenty of food and fills your hearts with joy" (Acts 14:17). God's provisions are gifts; we don't deserve them or earn them. "He causes his sun to rise on the evil and the good, and sends rain on the righteous and the unrighteous," said Jesus (Matt. 5:45).

These provisions are God's gift to us. How we use them is our gift to Him. God is certainly not to be blamed for the economic and ecological problems that threaten us today. Had mankind followed the principles given by God, many of these problems could have been avoided. Fallen man is trying to manage a fallen creation, a creation in "travail," and he simply can't do a successful job without God's wisdom and help.

God shows that He cares by providing for us. He also shows that He cares by His providential working in this world.

Providence is, I admit, an old-fashioned word; but it's still a good word. It comes from the Latin and means "to see beforehand." God is never caught by surprise; He goes before and prepares the way. Providence is that marvelous working of God so that all of the events in His universe accomplish the purposes He has in mind. "The LORD has established his throne in heaven, and his kingdom rules over all" (Ps. 103:19). That doesn't describe a "limited God" in the process of becoming infinite!

It's because of God's providence that we can have promises that encourage us, because God is able to perform what He promises. His providence also is an encouragement to prayer; for, if He is *not* in control, there is no sense talking to Him about your needs. God "works out everything in conformity with the purpose of his will" (Eph. 1:11), even though you and I don't always fully understand what He is doing or why He is doing it. To believe otherwise is to put yourself into an unorganized universe that operates on the frightening basis of haphazard chance.

This explains why God's people avoid using the words "luck" and "fate," because neither word belongs in the vocabulary of the person who trusts a God big enough to rule the universe.

God cares for us in the same way we care for one another. He provides for us, He plans ahead and providentially works His plan, and He speaks to us to assure us. After my auto accident, when I woke up in the intensive care ward, one verse from the Bible kept echoing in my mind: "Great is the LORD, and greatly to be praised; and his greatness is unsearchable" (Ps. 145:3 KJV). God was speaking to me and reminding me that He was great enough to handle the situation!

Each time my wife and I have had a "crisis decision" in our lives, God has given us a definite word from the Scriptures, a promise to assure us. I have discovered that this has been the experience of many of God's people. In fact, one couple my wife and I are close to keeps a diary of the Bible promises God has given them in times of difficulty and trial—and they have had their share, believe me!

Now, we must be careful how we use the Bible when we are going through trials. Unless we are reading God's Word regularly, listening daily to His voice, we aren't likely to hear Him say much when the roof caves in on us. Nor will he say much to us if we just reach for the Bible and open it at random. (A friend of mine calls that practice "religious roulette.") The child who is in good fellowship with his parents when the sun is shining will find their presence and words even more meaningful in the darkness. God's promises aren't celestial life preservers that He throws out to strangers in the storm. They are expressions of His love and care, given to His children who walk with Him and seek to obey Him.

However, it's when we are going through difficulties that God's promises take on new meaning for us. The famous British preacher Charles Spurgeon used to say that the promises of God never shine so brightly as in the furnace of affliction; and this is true. Scriptures we have known from childhood suddenly become fresh and exciting when we read them through our tears and in our pain.

Just recently, I leafed through several of my Bibles, and I noted again the dates written in the margins next to certain verses. Only the Lord and I know what happened on those days and why those verses were especially meaningful at that time. I can bear witness to the fact that my Father in heaven has always had an encouraging word for me each time I have needed it. He cares for us by speaking to us and sharing His promises.

But promises are effective only if you *know* them and *trust* them. That's why it's important for God's people to read the Bible and get to understand the heart and mind of God. But we also need to *believe* God's promises and claim them for ourselves. "For no matter how many promises God has made, they are 'Yes' in Christ. And so through him the 'Amen' is spoken by us to the glory of God" (2 Cor. 1:20). God's promise is His "Yes!" and our "Amen" is our "Yes!" to His promise. It is our faith that releases the power in God's promises.

Again, let me remind you that I'm not describing a "crisis relationship" with God. I'm describing a daily relationship that deepens as we fellowship with God in prayer and in meditation on His Word. I'm not suggesting that God won't meet the needs in a crisis of those who usually neglect Him; but that's not the best approach. We will have an easier time trusting God in the darkness if we have walked with Him in the light.

"Cast all your anxiety on him because he cares for you" (1 Pet. 5:7). That's a great promise! I like the way J. B. Phillips translates it: "You can rest the weight of all your anxieties upon Him, for you are always in His care."

How do we do this?

To begin with, we must have this personal relationship with God through faith in Jesus Christ. We must know that He is our Father and Christ is our Savior.

Then, we must be willing to admit that we can't handle our problems without divine help. In the verses just preceding, Peter writes: "'God opposes the proud but gives grace to the humble.'

Humble yourselves, therefore, under God's mighty hand, that he may lift you up in due time" (1 Pet. 5:5–6).

Once and for all, we must surrender ourselves, our problems, and our anxieties to the Lord. This is a step of faith. We claim His promise, give ourselves to Him, and trust Him to keep His word. We do this, not to escape life, but that God might help us face life. It's amazing what relief comes to your heart when you turn the controls over to Him. A new power, along with a new hope, takes over in your life.

Finally, we keep in touch with the Father through prayer, times of meditation, and the reading of the Scriptures. The crisis of dedication leads to the process of devotion.

What does God do for those who sincerely surrender themselves into His hands day by day?

To begin with, when you "cast all your anxiety on him," God gives you *the courage to face life honestly*. We need that, because our tendency is either to try to run away or to begin to get bitter. When bad things happen, some people reach for the bottle, or the needle; and then when they wake up, the problems are still there, but they're in worse shape to handle them. God gives the courage we need to face the situation honestly and not try to escape it.

"Facing the situation honestly" may include having to accept handicap, suffering, even death. If we want to enjoy the blessings of life, we must also be willing to accept the burdens that come with them. The same little child that rejoices our hearts can also break our hearts. This is the way life operates, and to fight against it is only to hurt ourselves and the people around us.

One of the most courageous couples I ever met were members of a church where I was pastor. Years before I arrived on the scene, their little boy had contracted a brain disease that left him an invalid. He spent his entire life in bed, unable to speak, read, or use his hands creatively. When I first visited in the home, the boy had become a man; but he was still lying in bed, wearing diapers, and he needed to have someone with him constantly.

"Pastor, don't feel sorry for us because of Kenny," his parents told me. "People think he's a burden, but to us, he's a blessing from God. We've learned so much about God's grace in taking care of Kenny."

When you cast yourself and your anxieties on the Lord, He not only gives you the courage to face life honestly, but He also gives you *the wisdom to understand what needs to be done*. This doesn't mean He hands us an operations manual that explains why everything has happened as it did and what purposes the Father plans to achieve. God usually guides us a step at a time, a day at a time. We don't hear any voices or have any visions, but somehow we seem to know what He wants us to do.

Here is a promise that my wife and I have claimed many times, and it has never failed: "If any of you lacks wisdom, he should ask God, who gives generously to all without finding fault, and it will be given to him" (James 1:5). Instead of running around aimlessly, blaming this one and begging from that one, the child of God quietly waits before the Father for direction in the decisions of life. This doesn't mean we ignore the counsel of others, because often God uses other people to guide us; but even that experience comes because we are waiting on the Lord.

Third, when you cast all your anxieties on the Lord, He gives you *the strength to do what He wants you to do*. "I can do everything through Him who gives me strength" (Phil. 4:13). J. B. Phillips has caught the excitement of this promise in his translation: "I am ready for anything through the strength of the One who lives within me."

All of nature depends on hidden resources. God's people also depend on divine resources that are hidden to the human eye. We have our roots in the eternal. "He who dwells in the shelter of the Most High will rest in the shadow of the Almighty. I will say of the LORD, 'He is my refuge and my fortress, my God, in whom I trust'" (Ps. 91:1–2). "God is our refuge and strength, an ever present help in trouble" (Ps. 46:1).

A divine strength is given to those who yield themselves to the Father and obey what He tells them to do. Down through the ages, the prophets and the saints have given witness to the fact that God helps those who trust Him; and I've seen this same witness borne by hundreds of "garden variety" believers who have been called to suffer in one way or another.

God gives you the courage to face life honestly, the wisdom to understand what He wants you to do, and the strength to do it. The fourth ministry He performs for those who cast their cares on Him is this: He gives you *the faith to be patient while He works out His perfect will in your life.* How many times I've quoted Psalm 37:5 to myself and to those under my ministry: "Commit your way to the LORD, trust also in him, and He will do it" (NASB).

It takes faith to be patient, but it also takes trials to give us that patience! Trials without faith will create impatience, but trials *plus faith* can create in us a patience that permits God to do what He wants to do. I have a tendency to become impatient and to want to rush ahead and do things my way. "Be still, and know that I am God" (Ps. 46:10) is a statement that has often rebuked me. The Hebrew word translated "Be still" literally means, "Be relaxed. Take your hands off!"

God meets our needs, not by working *instead* of us or *in spite* of us, but by working in us, through us, and for us. So long as we love Him and seek to fulfill His purposes, He causes all things—even seeming tragedies—to work together for good. "And we know that in all things God works for the good of those who love him, who have been called according to his purpose" (Rom. 8:28).

How can we be sure that God cares?

The entire universe is constant proof of His provision for us. The God who gives the flowers their beauty and the birds their daily food also gives His people all that they need, just when they need it.

God is providentially at work in this world and in our lives. The events of life are appointments, not accidents, as He works out His perfect plan.

God has given us His promises to assure us and encourage us in the dark days of life. The words that God gave to Israel through Moses are alive with power for God's people today: "Be strong and courageous. Do not be afraid or terrified because of them [your enemies], for the LORD your God goes with you; he will never leave you nor forsake you" (Deut. 31:6).

But the greatest proof that God cares for you is what He did on a cross outside the walls of Jerusalem.

God's greatest—and final—answer to human suffering and the presence of evil in this world is: Calvary.

The God Who Suffers

A group of Christian missionaries visited Mahatma Gandhi to discuss their work in India. Before they left, Gandhi asked them to sing for him one of their Christian hymns. "Which one shall we sing?" they asked.

"Sing the one that best expresses what you believe," he replied. They sang together:

> When I survey the wondrous cross
> On which the Prince of glory died,
> My richest gain I count but loss,
> And pour contempt on all my pride.

We today take for granted the symbol of the cross. We forget that, in Jesus' day, the cross was a despicable thing, reserved for the vilest offenders society could condemn. Nobody in the Roman Empire would have written a song about the cross, any more than we today would write a hymn about the gas chamber, the electric chair, or the gallows.

Jesus Christ not only did something *on* the cross, but He did something *to* the cross! He transformed it from a symbol of suffering to a symbol of victory and glory. And regardless of what a person may think about Jesus Christ, anyone who seriously examines the subject of suffering must confront Calvary. "He, as no other, stands before our eyes as an example and a warning," wrote Sholem Asch, "and demands of us, harries us, prods us to follow his example and carry out his teachings."

When you read the four Gospels, you discover a remarkable thing: Jesus didn't explain suffering, but rather experienced it and did all He could to relieve it. Through His life, death, and resurrection, He transformed suffering *and* the cross on which He suffered and died. So powerful was His impact that, twenty years or so after the crucifixion, Paul was able to write, "May I never boast except in the cross of our Lord Jesus Christ" (Gal. 6:14). In the Roman Empire, crucifixion was never mentioned in polite society; yet here is Paul *boasting* in the cross!

If there is one clear message that Jesus gives us about God and suffering, it is this: God is identified with us in our suffering and can enable us to turn tragedy into triumph. When you and I are fighting the battle, or facing the furnace, God is not a disinterested spectator; He is an active participant with us in the sufferings of life. "In all their distress he too was distressed, and the angel of his presence saved them" (Isa. 63:9).

The God of the Bible, the God of Abraham, Isaac, and Jacob, the God and Father of our Lord Jesus Christ, is not the "Unmoved Mover" of the philosophers. When He revealed Himself to Moses at the burning bush, He said: "I have indeed seen the misery of my people in Egypt. I have heard them crying out because of their slave drivers, and I am concerned about their suffering" (Exod. 3:7). During the difficult days of the judges, the Lord again assured His people by raising up deliverers, "For the LORD had compassion on them as they groaned under those who oppressed and afflicted them" (Judg. 2:18).

In the life and ministry of Jesus Christ, we see most clearly God's concern for His people and for all suffering humanity. Born into a poor home, Jesus knew the meaning of poverty and sacrifice. He labored as a carpenter. He was part of a hated race, and He lived at a time when Palestine was a police state. He hungered and thirsted, He grew weary, He wept, and He died. He was arrested and deprived of His rights, convicted on a trumped-up charge, and nailed to a cross. Nobody could ever accuse Jesus of Nazareth of being an unconcerned spectator in the drama of life!

Why did He endure all of this? For one thing, He was showing us the heart of a loving God. "Anyone who has seen me has seen the Father" (John 14:9). When you look at Jesus in the Gospel records, you see God with a child in His arms, God with tears in His eyes, God breaking bread for hungry peasants, God bleeding and dying for a needy world. Jesus is a most convincing argument that God cares.

His sufferings on earth had another purpose: they prepared Him to identify with our sufferings today. "Because he himself suffered when he was tempted, he is able to help those who are being tempted" (Heb. 2:18). "For we do not have a high priest who is unable to sympathize with our weaknesses, but we have one who has been tempted in every way, just as we are—yet was without sin. Let us then approach the throne of grace with confidence, so that we may receive mercy and find grace to help in our time of need" (Heb. 4:15–16).

I understand the perplexity of those who honestly confess, "We don't understand what it means for God to suffer." We're so prone to identify suffering with pain—physical feelings—that we are baffled to think that God, who is Spirit, could ever feel pain. We understand Jesus feeling pain, because He joined His divine nature to human nature and became a man. But God?

At the same time, however, the people who question God's ability to suffer have no problem with God's ability to *love*. Anyone who has ever loved in a mature way knows that love involves suffering. Certainly sympathy is a part of love. In fact, the purer the love, the greater the possibility for suffering. God's suffering in no way affects His supreme joy, nor does it add to or take from his divine nature. Jesus was no less the Son of God when He was weeping than when He was preaching a sermon.

In fact, even God's judgments and disciplines are proofs that He cares. "My son, do not make light of the Lord's discipline, and do not lose heart when he rebukes you, because the Lord disciplines those he loves, and punishes everyone he accepts as a son" (Heb. 12:5–6). A friend of mine, who works with wayward teenagers, tells me that their first step toward rebellion was lack of discipline on the part of their parents. "If they cared for us," the teens tell him, "they would have disciplined us and stopped us from trying to rebel." Our Father in heaven will never *harm* us, but He will hurt us in order to keep us from harming ourselves.

The greatest proof that God loves us is the cross of Jesus Christ. "But God demonstrates his own love for us in this: While we were still sinners, Christ died for us" (Rom. 5:8). God subjected Himself to the same laws of the universe that man is subjected to. Dorothy Sayers states it clearly:

> That for whatever reason God chose to make man as he is— limited and suffering and subject to sorrows and death—He had the honesty and the courage to take His own medicine. Whatever game He is playing with His creation, He has kept His own rules and played fair.

The word *fair* usually comes into discussions about pain and tragedy. "It isn't fair that our son should be killed!" says an angry mother. "I was just ready for retirement and my wife dropped dead!" says a bewildered husband. "It just isn't fair!"

Was it "fair" for Jesus to be slandered, lied about, arrested on false charges, mocked, abused, brutally whipped, publicly humiliated, and then crucified like the lowest thief? Of course not! Yet He willingly accepted the cup the Father prepared for Him because he knew it was the only way the problem of suffering and evil in the world could finally be solved.

What does the cross of Jesus Christ teach us about suffering? To begin with, the cross makes it clear that *suffering and love are not incompatible*. The Father loves the Son, and yet the Father willed that the Son die on a cross. Jesus never once questioned His Father's love. "This is love: not that we loved God, but that he loved us and sent his Son as an atoning sacrifice for our sins" (1 John 4:10).

"God has forsaken me and doesn't love me anymore," a dear elderly saint said to me when I visited her in the hospital. "If He loved me, He wouldn't let me suffer like this."

"I wonder if the Father loved Jesus when He was suffering on the cross?" I asked.

"Of course He did!" she answered in a flash. Then she smiled and said, "Yes, I'm sure God loves me—*but it still hurts!*"

The cross teaches us a second lesson: *Suffering is not always punishment for our sins.* Being fallen creatures as we are, when tragedy strikes, we immediately feel guilty and start figuring out what sins of commission or omission God is punishing! But that kind of logic cannot be applied to Calvary. "He committed no sin, and no deceit was found in his mouth" (1 Pet. 2:22). He was there, not because of His sins, for He had none, but because of *our* sins. "He himself bore our sins in his body on the tree" (1 Pet. 2:24).

We have learned that a part of our suffering comes from the fact that we live in a "groaning" world. Because of sin, creation is in bondage and travail. God had to judge His own creation when man sinned. He called for thorns to grow out of the ground. He decreed that man would live by the sweat of his brow, and that man would one day return to dust. *Jesus identified Himself with these judgments.* In the Garden, He "prayed more earnestly, and his sweat was like drops of blood falling to the ground" (Luke 22:44). He wore a crown of thorns, and He died, experiencing the full impact of what it means to be a part of "the dust of death" (Ps. 22:15). When He died, all of nature seemed to sympathize with Him; for the sun was darkened, there was an earthquake, and some of the graves were opened.

Our modern world has gotten soft on sin, so much so that it was a psychiatrist, not an evangelist, who wrote the book *What Ever Became of Sin?* We're so accustomed to seeing criminals go free and politicians whitewashed, we don't think sin is worth worrying about. After all, *we* aren't as guilty as the people we see on TV, so surely the Lord won't be too hard on us!

100

Sin is not a negative thing, the mere absence of good. Sin is a positive force—an evil force—in the world today; and a holy God must hate sin. God can transform suffering into glory, but *He cannot transform sin.* He must judge it, and that is what He did on the cross. How it happened, we cannot explain, but the Bible affirms that it is true. When Jesus died on the cross, He died for the sins of all the world. In some mysterious manner, He became the sinless substitute for the guilty world.

What does this mean to us as far as our suffering is concerned? It means that *nobody can ever accuse God of not caring.* As Dorothy Sayers expressed it, God "took His own medicine." And when He did, He once and for all dealt with the power of evil in the world. Furthermore, He released in Jesus Christ the only power available that can transform suffering into glory.

There is something worse than suffering, and that is sin. Don't pity Jesus on the cross. Instead, pity Caiaphas, the scheming religious liar; or Pilate, the spineless Roman politician; or Judas, the money-grabbing thief who wasted the opportunity of a lifetime. We shed tears, and rightly so, for a loved one killed in an accident; but too often we don't weep for the drunken driver who caused the death. We permit our suffering to blind us to the real cause of suffering in this world—man's rebellion against God.

This leads us to a third important truth: The cross teaches us that *suffering can accomplish purposes for others.* Joseph suffered that he might be able to save his family. Moses suffered that he might be able to lead his people to freedom. David suffered that he might be able to establish a righteous kingdom in Israel. The prophets suffered that they might deliver God's truth to a sinning nation. Jesus suffered that He might "save his people from their sins" (Matt. 1:21).

None of us can suffer for others in the same way Jesus suffered, that is, as a sinless substitute to accomplish their redemption. But we can suffer in the will of God on behalf of others and, through the power of God, help to change their lives. There is something about a person *voluntarily* suffering, even suffering *unjustly*, that releases the power of God and helps accomplish wonderful things in the character of those who are involved. It's a marvelous day in a family when the children realize that parental love *costs something*. "Greater love has no one than this, that one lay down his life for his friends" (John 15:13).

There are times, then, when we suffer as Jesus suffered—for the sake of others. This turns suffering into ministry and it sanctifies the pain that we must bear. The cross reminds us that there is no higher calling than this, that God should use our suffering to be a help and blessing to others. This is probably what Jesus had in mind when He said, "If anyone would come after me, he must deny himself and take up his cross and follow me" (Mark 8:34).

Our Lord's cross assures us that *suffering in God's will always leads to glory*. I want to make it clear that suffering *of itself* does not automatically lead to glory. It leads to glory only if we are in the will of God and depending on the grace of God. Good Friday, a day of humiliation, was followed by Easter Sunday, a day of exaltation, because Jesus did the will of God.

By His sufferings, death, and resurrection, Jesus has transformed the cross from a base weapon of human cruelty to a divine tool for heavenly ministry. The cross used to symbolize shame, but now it symbolizes glory. It was once identified with weakness, but now it is identified with strength. The cross does not deny the reality of human suffering; it transforms it.

When our Lord was hanging on the cross, He made seven remarkable statements. While these statements have a great deal to say about God's salvation for man, they also reveal something about how we can, because of the cross, handle human suffering.

"*Father, forgive them, for they do not know what they are doing*" (Luke 23:34). There was no bitterness in the heart of Jesus against those who were causing His pain. Bitterness only makes suffering worse and closes the spiritual channels through which God can pour His grace. Sometimes when we suffer, we need to forgive those who are not suffering, or perhaps those who are (like Job's comforters) trying to tell us why we are suffering.

"*I tell you the truth, today you will be with me in paradise*" (Luke 23:43). Jesus spoke these words to a believing criminal, hanging on an adjacent cross. Suffering can make us very selfish; but Jesus thought of others. He gave hope to a condemned man.

"*Dear woman, here is your son. . . . Here is your mother*" (John 19:26–27). He spoke these words to His mother, Mary, and His disciple, John. Our suffering shouldn't hinder us from caring for the normal responsibilities of life if we can. We must care for those whom we love.

"*My God, my God, why have you forsaken me?*" (Matt. 27:46). He cried these words when the cross was shrouded in darkness. There are times of darkness and loneliness when we suffer. There are hours of anguish and isolation. But they are followed by times of closer fellowship with God. Jesus was forsaken for a moment that we might never be forsaken.

"*I am thirsty*" (John 19:28). The only way to escape the normal human pains of life is to cease being human. Jesus experienced need, and others had to meet that need by giving Him a drink. Our suffering often makes us feel helpless; we resent being cared for like little children. But our Savior was willing for an anonymous bystander to wet His lips. He served others by permitting them to serve Him. When someone gives us a cup of cold water in Jesus' name, he is giving it to the Savior (Matt. 25:40).

"It is finished!" (John 19:30). His suffering was not in vain. He accomplished the work the Father gave Him to do. Our suffering is not in vain, if we dedicate it to Him and seek to use it for His glory. We may not always understand the purposes God is accomplishing; but if we cooperate and trust, He will achieve His goals, and we will share in the reward.

"Father, into your hands I commit my spirit" (Luke 23:46). Suffering doesn't last forever, and death is not the end. When God's people suffer, the Father is near them, sharing their pain. Jesus died the way He lived—yielded into the hands of God. Our suffering may end in death, or it may end in healing. Either way, we are in the Father's hands.

This leads us to the final lesson we may learn about suffering from the cross: *creative suffering demands that we surrender to God.* I think it's significant that Jesus died on *a cross.* The Jews used stoning for capital offenses, and the Romans often beheaded criminals; but Jesus died on a cross. *Crucifixion is one form of death you cannot inflict on yourself.* It demands total surrender on the part of the one being crucified.

While angry resistance may be a normal response to pain and loss, we dare not maintain that attitude, or we will only destroy ourselves and rob ourselves of the enrichment God has planned for us. For God's people, surrender is not fatalistic resignation to a cruel master. Rather, it is loving submission to a gracious

Father. Resignation means we are "giving in" but still fighting God down inside. Surrender means we have accepted His will and are trusting His power to see us through. Surrender doesn't mean that we give up the struggle; it means rather that we give up trying to struggle in our own wisdom and strength. We lean on Him.

Two vivid symbols illustrate the difference between fighting God's will and accepting God's will: the sword in Peter's hand and the cup in Jesus' hand. It may seem courageous for us to defy God and let everybody know that we are the master of our fate and the captain of our soul; but that approach to suffering only makes matters worse. We are no less courageous by submitting, because it takes a great deal of courage to put your life into the hands of another, especially when you're not sure what the overall plan really is. If we take the sword, we will perish; if we drink the cup, we will triumph.

Pleasure and protection from pain are not the most important things in life. Jesus deliberately put Himself into situations that brought Him suffering in one way or another. His most important task in life was to do the will of God, no matter what the cost might be.

The resurrection of Jesus Christ is God's evidence that what happened on the cross was finished, accepted, and triumphant. We must always look at the cross through the vantage point of the empty tomb. Together, the tree and the tomb say to us, "Your suffering is not in vain!"

What will it be for you: the sword or the cup?

When Life Falls Apart, How Do You Pray?

A dear friend of ours found herself in a sea of troubles. Her husband had gone blind, and then had come down with an incurable disease. She had a slight stroke that forced her to retire from her secretarial job and become a full-time "seeing-eye wife." Although they had many friends, they had no children.

Attempting to encourage her one day, I said, "I want you to know that we're praying for you."

"I appreciate that," she replied. "What are you praying for God to do?"

As she waited for my reply, I found myself struggling for a mature answer. I had never really been confronted with the question before! After all, when people are suffering, you pray for healing (if it's God's will), for strength, for special mercy in pain, and so on; and this is what I told her.

"Thank you," she said, "but please pray for one more request. *Pray that I won't waste all of this suffering.*"

For the first time in my ministry, it struck me that our times of suffering may become times of investment, *if* we learn how to pray about them. Perhaps the most important thing we can do is pray; but too often we don't really know *how* to pray. In fact, there may be times when our prayers seem futile and God appears to be deaf. It has been my experience as a pastor that unanswered prayers in times of suffering have caused more people to doubt God's power and goodness than perhaps any other experience.

We're going to learn from an experience the apostle Paul had when he prayed about his suffering; but first, I think it would be helpful if we tackled some of the so-called intellectual problems that some people have about prayer. Frankly, I've been studying the subject of prayer for years, and there are many questions that I cannot answer—nor can anybody else. I'm not discouraged by what I *don't* know about prayer because I'm too encouraged by what I *do* know about prayer.

If that statement bothers you, just keep in mind that it expresses just what today's scientists are saying as they study and apply the laws written into our universe. There are many things they don't know about the atom, but they find themselves making progress as they act upon what they do know. One day they operate on the basis of the "wave theory" of light, and the next day on the basis of the "particle theory." Anybody who claims that the "laws of nature" are set in concrete is reading an old textbook and had better get a new one.

This principle helps us to answer the pseudoscientific argument, "Prayer doesn't work because, if it did, it would violate the laws of nature." A man told me that one day as we were flying to Chicago, and all the while he was arguing, that huge jet was violating the laws of nature! God answers prayer, not by breaking His own laws, but by bringing into play higher laws that we don't fully understand.

"Don't get the idea that I'm against prayer!" I often hear these skeptics argue. "I think that it does people good to pray, even if God—if there is a God—doesn't answer."

But how can it do a person "good" to be involved in a religious lie? What possible benefit can come from a suffering person praying to himself? No doubt there are people who "feel good" after this kind of praying, but they would feel just as good if they sat and talked to their neighbor. The purpose of prayer is not for me to *feel* good, but to *be* good; and character cannot be built on deception. There certainly are "reflexive results" from prayer, but that's not the most important thing. The important thing is that prayer puts us in touch with God, and that means that His power is available to us as we struggle with the burdens of life.

Before we look at Paul's experience, let me remind you that true prayer is much more than asking God to give us what we think we need. We have every right to tell Him what we think we need, but we don't come to His throne to make demands. *It has well been said that the purpose of prayer is not to get man's will done in heaven, but to get God's will done on earth.* I have lived long enough to be thankful for unanswered prayer, and also to know the importance of following the example of Jesus when He prayed, "Father, if you are willing, take this cup from me; yet not my will, but yours be done" (Luke 22:42).

Now let's listen to Paul and learn how to pray about our suffering.

To keep me from becoming conceited because of these surpass-ingly great revelations, there was given me a thorn in my flesh, a messenger of Satan, to torment me. Three times I pleaded with the Lord to take it away from me. But he said to me, "My grace is sufficient for you, for my power is made perfect in weakness." Therefore I will boast all the more gladly about my weaknesses, so that Christ's power may rest on me. That is why, for Christ's sake, I delight in weaknesses, in insults, in hardships, in perse-cutions, in difficulties. For when I am weak, then I am strong. (2 Cor. 12:7–10)

God had permitted Paul to have spiritual experiences above and beyond anything any other believer had ever known. But with these experiences there came the danger of pride; so God had to balance them to keep Paul from failing. In one sense, it was the story of Job all over again: God permitted Satan to torment Paul and thus to keep him humble. We don't know exactly what Paul's "thorn in the flesh" was, nor is there any need for us to know. Whatever it was, it made Paul suffer; and, lurking in the shadows was the temptation for Paul to cut back on his ministry because of his physical affliction.

How do we pray about suffering? As I see it, there are three possible approaches.

To begin with, we can pray to *escape suffering*. This is a normal response and nobody would criticize us for doing it. Paul prayed three times—as Jesus did in the Garden—that the thorn might be removed. He doesn't tell us, but perhaps Paul even consulted his good friend Dr. Luke to see if there were God-given means available to help ease his pain or remove his affliction. I see nothing wrong with making use of the resources God has given us for our own physical well-being. When King

Hezekiah was sick, the prophet Isaiah told them to apply a poultice to the infection; and the king recovered.

We must remember that Paul was a Jew by birth, a member of the covenant nation. God had made some special promises to the Jews with reference to physical and material blessings. If the nation obeyed Him and observed His laws, He would provide them rain in season, He would give them abundant harvests, their flocks and herds would multiply, their families would increase, and their enemies would be defeated. "The LORD will keep you free from every disease" was also a part of the agreement (Deut. 7:7–16). What a marvelous basis for a prayer for healing!

But does God give His people that same basis for prayer today? And why did God give Israel those promises to begin with?

Let me answer these two questions by sharing an experience I had in a private hospital while visiting a cancer patient. When I walked into the room, I found her crying. She had just opened her mail and should have been enjoying the many expressions of love her friends had sent to her. Instead, she was crying and in her hand was a booklet.

Trying to smile, she took my hand and said, "Pastor, you couldn't have come at a better time. Look at this!" And she handed me the booklet. I've forgotten the title, but the theme was "divine healing." The author was trying to prove that God *always* heals when we have faith, because this is what He has promised in the Bible.

"Let's go through this book and check the Scriptures that he quotes," I suggested. As we did, we noticed an interesting thing; most of the "healing" quotations were from the Old Testament. When the author did quote the New Testament, the verses did

111

not specifically mention healing, and, if they did, they were citations from the Old Testament. God promised healing and prosperity to Israel, but He never gave those promises to the New Testament church.

I explained to my friend why God made those promises to the people of Israel. They were in the infancy of their nationhood and, like all children, had to learn primarily through rewards and punishments. God's promise was, "If you obey me, I will bless you. If you disobey me, I will chasten you." But there comes a time when children must learn to obey, not because obedience is *profitable*, but because obedience is *right*. They must obey from inward constraint, from love, and not from outward compulsion and fear.

When Jesus came to fulfill the Old Testament promises, it meant that the nation of Israel had come of age. "But when the time had fully come, God sent his Son, born of a woman, born under law, to redeem those under law, that we might receive the full rights of sons" (Gal. 4:4–5). There is a difference between "children" and "sons." Children are immature and must be controlled by rewards and punishments. Sons are mature and have the privilege of freedom, because their "controls" are within their hearts. Outward discipline has become inward character.

While it is normal and natural for us to pray to escape suffering, we must be careful not to tell God that He is *obligated* to answer our prayer. God's character and principles of working don't change from age to age, but His methods of dealing with His people do change. His goal for His people is maturity; He wants us to be mature sons and daughters, not immature children who must constantly be rewarded or punished. God wants

112

children who obey Him because they love Him, not because they hope to get some gift from Him.

We're back at Job's ash heap! It was Satan who accused Job of obeying God only because God had richly blessed him. Job's friends joined the accusation by agreeing with Satan; if Job would only confess his secret sins, God would bless him again. People today who urge suffering believers to "have more faith" or to "get right with God" are unconsciously agreeing with Satan and Job's friends. They are asking us to regress into childhood rather than grow into maturity.

Let me make it clear that God can impress an Old Testament promise on our hearts and give us the faith to believe that He will fulfill it. Even though all the promises in the Bible were not written *to* us, they were written *for* us; and God can apply them to our lives as He sees fit. But we must be sure that our faith is something He has sent down, not something that we have worked up. When people are suffering, it's easy to generate "emotional faith" and make exaggerated claims that later prove embarrassing.

God didn't answer Paul's prayer. The thorn was not removed. The apostle's prayer to escape suffering was unanswered. When this happens to some people, they get bitter against God; and this very bitterness is often proof that they were really not praying in faith at all. For faith puts us in contact with divine resources, and divine resources make it possible for us to turn disappointment into victory. If there is bitterness in the heart, there was probably first of all selfishness in the heart. We wanted our way, not God's way.

I was preaching in this vein one Sunday, and a man stopped me after the service to express his disagreement.

113

"Haven't you ever read Hebrews chapter 11?" he asked me. "Haven't you noticed the wonderful things God did for the people who trusted Him?"

I assured him that, indeed, I had read Hebrews 11 many times, and that I was fully aware of what God had done for the great men and women of faith whose names are recorded there. Then I asked him: "Have you ever noticed the word 'others' in that chapter?" I opened my Bible to Hebrews 11:35 and read to him: "Others were tortured and refused to be released. . . . Some faced jeers and flogging, while still others were chained and put in prison. They were stoned; they were sawed in two; they were put to death by the sword. They went about in sheepskins and goatskins, destitute, persecuted and mistreated."

"What's that got to do with it?" my accuser asked.

"Just this," I replied. "These people had just as much faith as the heroes mentioned in the first part of the chapter, *yet God didn't deliver them from their suffering!* Were they second-class citizens in God's kingdom?"

"I guess not," the man mumbled.

"You see, my friend," I explained, "sometimes our faith delivers us *from* difficulties, and sometimes it delivers us *in* difficulties. Either way, God honors our faith and He gets the glory. In fact, I'm inclined to believe that God can get greater glory at times by giving us grace to live with our suffering than by giving us power to escape it."

Our praying about suffering can take a second approach: We can pray to *endure suffering.* Paul was a Jew by birth, but he was a Roman by citizenship, and the Romans knew a great deal about endurance. When the *Titanic* was going down, the captain had time for only one brief message to his crew, and that was all that was needed: "Be British!" They knew what he meant. "Be Roman!" carried the same kind of impact in Paul's day.

The Romans were influenced by Stoic philosophy, which emphasized obedience to duty, courage, and indifference to pain. We know that Paul was acquainted with Stoic writings because he quoted two of their poets, Aratus and Cleanthes, in his address to the Greek philosophers on Mars Hill (Acts 17:28). We have every reason to believe that Paul was a courageous man, and that he could have learned to endure pain without complaining.

But the "endurance approach" presents some problems. To begin with, not everybody possesses the kind of inner strength that it takes to be a Stoic. Each of us is different and we can't expect everybody to have the fortitude of a Paul or a Marcus Aurelius. I read about a young preacher who was orating at a rescue mission service, and at one point in his sermon, he decided to quote from Kipling's famous poem "If—." It begins:

> If you can keep your head when all about you
> Are losing theirs and blaming it on you. . . .

and continues:

> If you can force your heart and nerve and sinew
> To serve your turn long after they are gone. . . .

and concludes:

> Yours is the Earth and everything that's in it,
> And—which is more—you'll be a Man, my son!

No sooner did the preacher finish reading the poem when a man at the back of the mission—one of the few who was awake and sober—called out, "Yeah, *but what if you can't?*"

But even if you *can*, the "endurance approach" creates a second problem: it tends to glorify man instead of God. We are proud of *our* strength and courage! We are the captains of our fate! The reason God gave Paul his thorn in the flesh was to keep him from getting proud! Human endurance, as wonderful as it is, would not solve Paul's problem; it would only make it worse.

Another consideration is that we all have only a certain amount of inner strength and it doesn't take long to use it up. If I'm using all my inner strength just to endure my suffering, then I'll have nothing left to give to daily living. One of the problems with the humanistic approach to life is that it does not allow for resources outside of man himself. What do you do when those resources run out? If I'm channeling all of my strength into endurance, then where do I find the power to care for my wife and children, to be kind to my neighbors, and to make my contribution to life?

Finally, the endurance approach can lead to a subtle kind of hypocrisy: we put up a "good front" when people are watching, and then fall apart when solitude rescues us. Apart from the fact that someday we may get our signals confused and get caught, there is the even greater problem of living a lie. The right use of suffering can build character, but a life of pretense can only erode character, even if our pretense is for the purpose of sheltering the people we love.

Endurance may be the only approach unbelievers can take to the problem of suffering, but God's people know a better way: we can pray to *enlist our suffering and make it work for us.*

If I pray to *escape* suffering, then I'm saying that suffering is my enemy and I must avoid it. But then I may be frustrating the plan of God. If I pray to *endure* suffering, I'm saying that suffering is my master; I'll find myself in bondage when God has created me to be free. If suffering is not to be either my enemy or my master, what is my relationship to suffering? The answer God gave to Paul is: *suffering must become your servant.*

In other words, if you pray to escape suffering, and God doesn't answer, don't pray simply to endure suffering. Pray to *enlist* your suffering. Make it work *for* you, not *against* you!

While I was recuperating from the auto accident I've already mentioned, I began to get typewritten letters from a total stranger who had heard about my experience. His letters were humorous, wise, and encouraging; and they opened up not only a correspondence, but a friendship. I discovered that the writer, George Hipshire, lived in a neighboring community, that he was blind, a diabetic, and that he had an artificial leg.

We chatted over the phone several times; and then, when I was well enough to drive again, I went to meet him personally. Our friendship deepened and often I would pick him up and we'd go out to lunch together. I get lost even in a parking lot, so George always had to give me directions to the different restaurants we frequented. It was literally a case of the blind leading the blind!

George was a remarkable fellow. He had every reason to give up on life, yet he had a zest for living that put healthy people to shame. (I should add that along with caring for his own needs, he was also caring for his aged mother!) He wrote excellent poetry; he played the piano fairly well and could carry a tune. He had an impish sense of humor that kept me on my toes. There was more than one occasion when this preacher went to encourage George only to return home carrying in his heart more encouragement than he left behind!

Later, the diabetes became worse, and George lost the other leg. This left him in a wheelchair, but it didn't diminish his spirit or limit his ministry. He still visited churches and civic groups, sharing songs and poems, and emphasizing his faith in Christ. If anybody gave evidence of pitying him, George would immediately set him straight. We had moved away from that area when George was called Home, but mutual friends tell me he went to glory triumphantly.

George Hipshire was not perfect. He had his "blue days" just like the rest of us. But the overriding impact of his life was that of joyful service for others. He had learned to enlist his suffering and make it work for him. I don't know if George ever heard about Harold Russell, who lost his hands in World War II and became a famous actor and author, as well as an encourager of the handicapped; but George certainly would have agreed with Russell's philosophy: "It is not what you have lost, but what you have left that counts."

How, then, do we go about *enlisting* our suffering so that it works for us and not against us? From Paul's experience, we can discover some of the steps that we can take.

First, we must accept our suffering as God's gift. "There was given me a thorn in my flesh," wrote Paul. What a strange gift! Let me remind you that acceptance is not resignation, giving up. Resignation is a passive attitude that borders on fatalism. Acceptance is active cooperation with God, *and it always includes gratitude.* I may not always be able to be thankful *for* what has happened, but I can be thankful *in* what has happened. It's the attitude of gratitude and acceptance that takes the poison out of suffering and keeps us from becoming bitter against God.

All of this, of course, is an act of faith, and it must come from the heart. If we aren't yet willing to accept what God has given us, we must then ask Him to "make us willing to be made willing." The longer we oppose God, the more opportunities we lose for receiving His blessings and ministering to others.

Second, we must surrender what He has given us back to Him. It is only when we see our experience as His gift to us that we can return it as our gift to Him. There is such a thing as placing our pain on the altar as an act of worship to the glory of God. God can sanctify pain just as easily as He can sanctify service, if we will let Him.

Third, we must listen for His message. At first, God said nothing to Paul, even though he had prayed fervently three times. But God's silence ought not to discourage us. Even when He is silent, He is suffering with us and preparing us for His special word. Finally, it came to Paul: "My grace is sufficient for you, for my power is made perfect in weakness." Paul learned how weak he was—and how strong God is! He discovered that God's grace and power were sufficient to enable him to enlist his suffering and make it work for him.

I said earlier that the fatal flaw in the humanistic approach to suffering is that it forces us to be self-contained and self-sufficient. While we can draw upon outside resources for physical strength, we are not allowed to draw upon outside resources for spiritual strength. But there comes a time when our own resources run out; then what do we do?

God's people have an inexhaustible supply of everything they need because of the grace of God. Our Father is "the God of all grace" (1 Pet. 5:10). The promise is that "he gives us more grace" (James 4:6). Grace means that whatever we receive, we don't deserve, earn, or merit. God's grace flows freely from His loving heart because of what Jesus Christ did for us on the cross.

When you know you are strong, you are weak; but when you know you are weak, you are strong. Our confession of weakness is not an admission of defeat. It's an application for victory! "For when I am weak," Paul confessed, "then I am strong."

We must accept our suffering as God's gift and then surrender it back to Him. We must listen for God's message and, as we do, depend on God's grace. Finally, *we must live for God's glory.* The key phrase in 2 Corinthians 12:10 is "for Christ's sake." "God, do not tell me why I suffer, for I am no doubt unworthy to know why," says an old Hasidic prayer, "but help me to believe that I suffer for Your sake."

God can bestow present glory from the sufferings of His people but he also promises *future* "praise, glory and honor when Jesus Christ is revealed" (1 Pet. 1:7). "For our light and momentary troubles are achieving for us an eternal glory that far outweighs them all" (2 Cor. 4:17).

When bad things come to God's people, they must by all means pray. But we must be careful lest we try to manipulate God into doing our will instead of His will. I ran across this statement by F. W. Robertson that perfectly summarizes what I have tried to say about prayer.

That life is most holy in which there is least of petition and desire, and most of waiting upon God; that in which petition most often passes into thanksgiving. Pray till prayer makes you forget your own wish, and leave it or merge it in God's will. The Divine wisdom has given us prayer, not as a means whereby to obtain the good things of earth, but as a means whereby we learn to do without them; not as a means whereby we escape evil, but as a means whereby we become strong to meet it.

Phillips Brooks would agree with him.

Do not pray for easy lives. Pray to be stronger men. Do not pray for tasks equal to your powers. Pray for powers equal to your tasks.

How suffering and God's grace can make us "stronger men and women" is the theme of our next chapter.

Character

The central challenge in our lives is not to explain suffering, but rather to be the kind of people who can face suffering and make it work for us and not against us. "If afflictions refine some, they consume others," said the Puritan preacher Thomas Fuller, and he was right. Nobody will deny that what happens *to* us is important. But what happens *in* us is also important, because that will help to determine what happens *through* us.

I'm speaking, of course, about character; and while I don't want this chapter to sound like a high school commencement address, I find I can't deal with suffering and honestly avoid the subject of character. Character is the raw material of life. "Man," said Alexis Carell, "is both the marble and the sculptor." Reputation is what you *think* I am, but character is what God and I *know* I am. There is a sense in which suffering helps to make a man or a woman; but there is also a sense in which suffering reveals what they are made of.

Some people deal with trials by running away, either physically or emotionally. They either reach for the car keys or a plane ticket, or they reach for a pill, a needle, or a bottle—or a gun. Others do nothing when tragedy strikes; they find themselves paralyzed. We have to take them by the hand like little children and try to lead them out of the maze.

Most people put up some kind of resistance, even if it's only complaining or shaking their fist at heaven. Resistance is better than the kind of resignation that gives up on God, life, other people, and any hope for improvement. At least the sufferer who is resisting is maintaining some kind of active control. It's when we become passive that the real trouble begins. A passive approach to suffering can never build character. Man must, with God's help, be the sculptor.

This means that our attitude must be one of *acceptance with a view to growth*. If we're going to get anything out of our trials, we have to put something into them. "Wherever souls are being tried and ripened, in whatever commonplace and homely way," said Phillips Brooks, "there God is hewing out the pillars for His temple." Whatever else a person may have, if he doesn't have character, he has nothing.

By itself, suffering cannot produce character. The same sun that melts the ice also hardens the clay. All of us need "outside help," and that help can come only from God. When David wrote Psalm 18 and looked back at those difficult years of persecution and exile, he said to God, "Thy providence makes me great" (Ps. 18:35 NEB). David possessed tremendous potential that could be released only by suffering and the grace of God.

The process by which God builds character is outlined in Romans 5:1–5.

> Therefore, since we have been justified through faith, we have peace with God through our Lord Jesus Christ, through whom we have gained access by faith into this grace in which we now stand. And we rejoice in the hope of the glory of God. Not only so, but we also rejoice in our sufferings, because we know that suffering produces perseverance; perseverance, character; and character, hope. And hope does not disappoint us, because God has poured out his love into our hearts by the Holy Spirit, whom he has given us.

The process by which God builds character into His people begins with suffering. The Greek word used here means "pressures, restrictions, confinement, being pressed together." It can describe outward troubles or inward anguish. The word was used to describe crushing the grapes and the olives in the presses.

Whether or not God can build character in this world apart from suffering is another hypothetical question that ought not to detain us. At least in the world we know, it takes trials to make something beautiful and useful out of the raw materials of life. The student's struggle with truth develops his intelligence; the athlete's struggle with his records and his opponents helps to develop his muscles and coordination; the musician's struggle with more difficult pieces develops his playing skill; and the soul's struggle with the trials of life helps to build character.

One reason, I think, is because the demands of life help us to develop discipline and mastery of ourselves. Most of what happens around us is beyond our control; *but we can control what happens within us.* Paul called this perseverance, which means "patient endurance, the ability to stay with it and not fall apart." "Better a patient man than a warrior, a man who controls his temper than one who takes a city" (Prov. 16:32).

This "brave endurance" in turn produces character. This word means "the quality of being approved." You have passed the test! Job had this in mind when he said, "But he knows the way that I take; when he has tested me, I will come forth as gold" (Job 23:10). When a prospector had his one sample tested by the assayer, the sample wasn't the important thing. The assayer's report was the important thing, for if it said that the sample was indeed gold, then the prospector was rich. The approval from the test opened up a whole mine of gold, far more valuable than the sample!

So it is with character that is built out of trial: it opens up to us the resources of God. The word translated "character" in Romans 5:4 was used in Paul's day to describe gold tested in the fire, as well as soldiers who proved themselves in battle. What a thrilling thing it is for a coach to watch a young athlete overcome new obstacles and develop new skills, or for an instructor to watch a musician discipline his body and conquer new challenges!

But does God have the right to make *other* people suffer just so He can help me develop my character? Isn't the price a bit too high? We can perhaps overlook the livestock, but we can't overlook the fact that all of Job's children and employees (with the exception of the messengers) were killed as a part of God's controversy with Satan. It was one thing for God to permit Satan to take away Job's wealth and health; but why must his children and workers lay down their lives just to make Job a better man? This approach to building character seems to make God irresponsible.

We must be very careful when we use the word *responsible* with reference to God. *Responsible to whom?* Certainly not to a higher power, because there can be no power higher than God. Responsible to His people? He is certainly responsible to keep His promises, but He has never promised us an easy life. And we want to be careful not to adopt Satan's philosophy of life that requires God to shelter us from trouble in return for our love and obedience.

Some claim they have seen the "wrong" people fall ill or get hurt or die young. While I confess that it is easy to *feel* that way, careful reflection tells me that this kind of thinking contributes nothing to the life of the person who hurts. In fact, it approaches the dangerous position of playing God in people's lives.

For, after all, if I have the ability to decide who the *wrong* people are—the people who are *not* supposed to get sick, be hurt, or die—then I also have the ability to decide who the *right* people are! Others may want to assume this awesome responsibility, but I, for one, will not be among them. I'm prepared to leave matters of life and death in the hands of God and agree with the declaration of faith that Abraham gave: "Will not the Judge of all the earth do right?" (Gen. 18:25).

To accuse God of wrongdoing because "innocent people" died in order that one man might develop his character is, I think, a bit presumptuous on anyone's part. Millions of wonderful men and women gave their lives in wars to bring about changes far less permanent, and yet we honor them for their sacrifice. Furthermore, it was not Job *alone* who was involved in this conflict: Job's experience has been a help and encouragement to millions of suffering people for many centuries. While we don't measure a man's painful experiences in terms of "satisfied customers," neither can we ignore the far-reaching effects of Job's ordeal.

When we start asking questions like "Why did God permit Job's ten innocent children to die in a tornado?" we are raising issues that create fog rather than sunshine. We have just as much right to ask, "Why were these children born at all if God knew that one day they'd be killed in a storm?" In Job's day, the birth of ten healthy children was considered a blessing; but whatever in this life can *bless* my heart can also *break* my heart. Job never raised either of these questions. He simply said, "The LORD gave and the LORD has taken away; may the name of the LORD be praised."

God knows the best tools to use in the shaping of our lives. Some people face harder tests in prosperity than in adversity. It has well been said that it is not easy to carry a full cup. We do know that God, in His love and wisdom, permits us to suffer, and that this suffering can produce patient endurance that, in turn, produces character. Our English word *character* actually comes from a Greek word that means "an engraving tool, a die for stamping an image." It's used only once in the New Testament when Jesus Christ is described in Hebrews 1:3 as "the exact representation" of God's being.

In other words, character doesn't come cheaply! The trials of life can be God's tools for engraving His image on our character. The experiences may not be enjoyable, but they can be profitable.

Paul affirms that character produces hope. In the Bible, "hope" is not "hope so," the attitude of the child at Christmas. Bible hope is *confidence in the future.* If we have proved the faithfulness of God in the afflictions of life, then we know He can handle whatever may lie ahead. In fact, "we rejoice in the hope of the glory of God" (Rom. 5:2). It's impossible in the will of God to separate suffering and glory! Persons of true godly character are neither optimists nor pessimists, but realists who have confidence in God.

The process for building character isn't an easy one, and so God has made provisions available to us to enable us to grow. These spiritual provisions belong to all of God's people because they have put their faith in Jesus Christ.

The first provision *is peace with God*. We have been accepted by God through Jesus Christ. At one time, we were God's enemies; but through the work of Christ on the cross, now we are reconciled to God (Rom. 5:10). That means that God is our Father and we are no longer at war with Him. When we were living our own lives, for our own pleasures, we were outside of God's will and everything was working against us. But now we are in His family, and He is making everything work together for us so that we might accomplish His purposes.

The second provision *is access to God*. "We have gained access by faith into this grace in which we now stand" (Rom. 5:2).

One of Job's major problems was his feeling that he had no access to God. "Why does the Almighty not set times for judgment?" he asked, suggesting that God ought to hold regular office hours for hearing complaints. "Why must those who know him look in vain for such days?" (Job 24:1). But Job's mistake was in wanting access to God so that he might tell God what to do, not find out what God wanted him to do.

Our access to God supplies us with God's grace, the spiritual resources we need to transform trials into triumphs. "God did not abolish the fact of evil: he transformed it," wrote Dorothy Sayers. "He did not stop the crucifixion: he rose from the dead."

We want God to solve the problems of suffering by the method of *substitution*—give us health instead of pain, wealth instead of poverty, friendship instead of loneliness—when His approach is to use the method of *transformation*. He transformed Paul's weakness into strength and his suffering into glory.

One of the most amazing women who ever served God and suffering humanity was Amy Carmichael. In 1895, she left a comfortable home in England and went to India as a missionary, and she remained there for the next fifty-six years! She risked her life to rescue little children from the superstitious bondage that destroyed them as "temple servants." In 1931, she suffered a serious fall and for the next twenty years was confined to her room. During that time, she was in almost constant pain, yet she managed the work of the mission and even wrote thirteen books! She wrote:

> We must learn to pray far more for spiritual victory than for protection from battle-wounds, relief from their havoc, rest from their pain. . . . This triumph is not deliverance from, but victory in, trial, and that not intermittent but perpetual.

The third provision is *the love of God*: "God has poured out his love into our hearts by the Holy Spirit, whom he has given us" (Rom. 5:5). God demonstrated His love at the cross when Jesus died for lost sinners, but he also shares His love with us personally. When I woke up in the intensive care ward after my auto accident, I found myself in pain, attached to numerous devices that were monitoring my hesitating functions, and yet *filled with the assurance of God's love*. Throughout those critical days, I experienced this love; and it was a great source of encouragement to me.

Love is a great force for building character. Love is personal and sacrificial. Love is patient. God can build galaxies by power alone, but it takes love to build people. Knowing that God loves us helps to take the poison out of pain and the selfishness out of suffering. It's not a feeling that we manufacture; rather, it's a gift that the Spirit shares within us.

God's people are indwelt by God's Spirit, and God's Spirit reproduces the character of God in our lives. "But the fruit of the Spirit is love, joy, peace, patience, kindness, goodness, faithfulness, gentleness and self-control" (Gal. 5:22–23). Some people, when they suffer, manifest selfishness and not love, complaining and not joy, restlessness and not peace. They are often impatient, unkind (especially to those who care for them), irritable, rude, and difficult to get along with. Why? Because they are giving in to their own feelings instead of surrendering to the Holy Spirit within them. Apart from His power, God's people can never build character out of affliction.

All of this leads to *freedom*, one of the greatest character blessings that can come out of anybody's suffering. When a person has faced and conquered affliction, he has developed the kind of character that makes for freedom. The pianist who has disciplined himself with the musical scales will one day have the freedom to improvise. The athlete who has exercised with discipline has the freedom to play the game and win. The artist or writer who has subjected himself to a master craftsman develops the freedom to create his own beauty.

Suffering is one tool God uses to develop the mature use of freedom. Puppets and robots don't suffer; people made in God's image do suffer. We are free to submit or free to rebel. How we respond will determine whether suffering will tear us down or build us up. If I give up, then suffering becomes my master and I lose my freedom. If I submit and trust God, suffering can become my servant and I will grow in my freedom.

I hope I haven't given you the idea that all of this is very easy, because it isn't. The things that matter most—like character—always cost the most. And I hope I haven't misled you into thinking that God's people never falter or fall in their experiences of affliction, because they do. We make mistakes, but we must keep going. Just when we think we've got things under control, a new problem emerges!

Yet, in the midst of all this trouble, we have peace with God, access to the grace of God, hope of the glory of God, and the inner witness of the love of God.

All of this is ours because of what Jesus Christ did at Calvary. He not only died for our sins, that we might become children of God; He also died for our sufferings, that we might be able to share the character and glory of God. And if He did all this for us when we were sinners and God's enemies, *how much more* will He do for us now that we are God's children!

"Why has God made me like this?" a suffering crippled woman asked her pastor.

Wisely he replied, "God has not made you—*He is making you!*"

The Craftsman is our loving Father. We are the raw material. Suffering is the tool. Character is the product.

10

You Never Suffer Alone

The sufferings that you and I experience will either involve us with others or isolate us from others. We will either build walls or bridges, depending on the attitude we take. I have watched people build walls of self-pity, resentment, bitterness, and unbelief; and, behind those walls, they have languished in loneliness, immaturity, and spiritual and emotional poverty.

On the other hand, I have seen suffering people build bridges and reach out with loving hands to others who hurt. I have seen these people mature and grow into a deeper fellowship with God and with their fellow man. Theirs has been an enriching and an encouraging experience because they thought of others. "We bereaved are not alone," wrote Helen Keller. "We belong to the largest company in all the world—the company of those who have known suffering. . . . So long as you can sweeten another's pain, life is not in vain."

The apostle Paul had this same thought in mind when he wrote the following words, which were born out of his own deep experience of affliction:

> Praise be to the God and Father of our Lord Jesus Christ, the Father of compassion and the God of all comfort, who comforts us in all our troubles, so that we can comfort those in any trouble with the comfort we ourselves have received from God. . . . We do not want you to be uninformed, brothers, about the hardships we suffered in the province of Asia. We were under great pressure, far beyond our ability to endure, so that we despaired even of life. Indeed, in our hearts we felt the sentence of death. But this happened that we might not rely on ourselves but on God, who raises the dead. He has delivered us from such a deadly peril, and he will deliver us. On him we have set our hope that he will continue to deliver us, as you help us by your prayers. (2 Cor. 1:3–4, 8–11)

It seems incredible that a great saint like Paul should despair of his life and almost give up! But he didn't give up, because he knew that God was with him and his friends were praying for him. Out of this experience, Paul gained a greater sensitivity to the pains of others, and he found himself better able to comfort them. He learned to shun self-pity and to look for opportunities to help somebody else who was in need. He tried to practice what he wrote in Romans 12:15, "Rejoice with those who rejoice; mourn with those who mourn."

When we suffer, it's easy to be selfish. Pleasure usually focuses on something outside ourselves, but pain is an "inside job." We can usually share our pleasures with others, but it's very difficult to share pain. If we aren't careful, we may find ourselves gradually being isolated from people; and this can lead to isolation from reality and from life. In times of affliction, we need others as much as others need us.

However, we don't want to give the kind of "comfort" that Job's friends gave to him! "Miserable comforters are you all!" Job told them (16:2). He also called them "worthless physicians" (13:4) who were wrong both in their diagnosis and their remedy. Job compared them to the wadis, the desert water-courses that are dry except during the rainy season. "A despairing man should have the devotion of his friends," said Job. "But my brothers are as undependable as intermittent streams . . . that cease to flow in the dry season, and in the heat vanish from their channels" (6:14–20).

Can't you just hear Job's sarcastic tone of voice as he says to his friends, "How you have helped the powerless! How you have saved the arm that is feeble! What advice you have offered to one without wisdom! And what great insight you have displayed!" (26:2–3).

We must give these men credit for at least keeping in touch with Job and knowing that he was in trouble. We also admire them for traveling long distances to share Job's trials with him. They sat in silence for a week and shared his sorrow. It isn't always necessary to talk in order to encourage someone. Just being there and caring is a great help to suffering people.

What went wrong? Why did these good friends turn out to be a part of the problem instead of a part of the solution? How can we learn from their mistakes and be better able to share God's love and comfort with hurting people?

Their first mistake was that *they reacted to Job's words instead of responding to Job's feelings.* Here was a man who was devastated by trouble, and they started an argument with him! Why? Because they were listening with the ears and not with the heart.

Suffering does strange things to people, even to mature godly people who really believe they can handle life. Pain breaks down a person's resistance, and this leads to fear. The sufferer begins to ask himself, "Am I losing control of my own life?" Fear leads to insecurity, and then everything becomes a threat to us. This helps to explain why suffering people sometimes become almost violent and turn on the very people they love. Unless you have had some experience of suffering, you may find it hard to accept what afflicted people say and do.

There's a reason why Job's friends were on the defensive: Job was a threat to them. These three men had their theology neatly packaged, and this gave them a feeling of security. But Job's experience not only unwrapped their neat package; it scattered the contents all over the ground! They could not explain why a godly man should suffer, and this meant that what happened to Job *might happen to them*!

God didn't call us to be prosecuting attorneys. He called us to be witnesses of His grace and comfort. God "comforts us in all our troubles, so that we can comfort those in any trouble with the comfort we ourselves have received from God" (2 Cor. 1:4). In our suffering, we must be channels, not reservoirs. We must share with others what God has done for us. If in my own trials, I have been open and honest with God, then I will have no problem letting others be open and honest with me when they suffer.

Nothing will test your own spiritual relationship with God like having to help somebody like Job! His friends had a very formal, businesslike relationship with God; and that relationship was shattered by Job's experiences and arguments. Their pat formulas, their oversimplified explanations, their cheap clichés all went down the drain in the presence of a man who challenged them to get to know God personally.

If you want to comfort others, let God first comfort you, and then share that comfort. But keep in mind that comfort is more than "sympathy." Our English word *comfort* comes from two Latin words that together mean "with strength." The Greek word Paul used means "to come alongside to help." Our word *encouragement* means "to put heart into." In other words, we comfort people, not by unanswerable arguments, but by unfailing love and acceptance.

This leads to the second mistake Job's friends made: *they explained instead of encouraged.* They turned Job's ash heap into a debating hall instead of a holy of holies. People who suffer do ask questions, but they are not always looking for answers. They are trying to find out if you and I are the kind of friends who will let them ask questions and not criticize them. They are testing us to see if we understand the feelings behind the questions. Job's friends never got that message. "Are all these words to go unanswered?" asked Zophar. "Is this talker to be vindicated?" (Job 11:2).

I said in the first chapter that people don't live on explanations; they live on promises. People have come to me with questions, and often I've had to reply, "Well, I don't know." This sometimes shocks them! But then I say, "I don't know the reason this happened to you, but I can give you some promises from God that can help you." In my earlier pastoral ministry, I felt I had to have an answer for everything; but now that I'm more mature, I have changed my mind. And I think I understand why. In those earlier years, I was protecting myself, like Job's three friends, and building my Christian life on simple formulas instead of on a growing relationship with God.

Quite frankly, there are no explanations for some of the things that happen in life; nor are we required to devise any. People need God far more than they need explanations. They need to trust the God that Paul met in his hour of suffering: "the Father of compassion and the God of all comfort" (2 Cor. 1:3). By caring for others, we show that God cares. (After all, God isn't likely to send an angel down to make the bed or carry the meal tray). When we listen, we're assuring others that God is listening. When we share His comfort, we are helping them to grow in their own personal relationship with God.

"But I've never been through what other people go through," we may argue. "How can I help them?"

The marvelous thing about God's comfort is that it is good medicine no matter what the ailment may be. God enables us to "comfort those *in any trouble* with the comfort we ourselves have received from God" (1 Cor. 1:4, italics added). Even if we have experienced trials similar to those of others, it's a dangerous thing to build on them, because no two experiences are exactly alike. In fact, one of the worst things we can do is to compare experiences with others, because it can end in subtle competition. People who hurt don't really believe that anybody else has felt exactly what they feel.

The best thing to do in comforting others is just to focus on God, the God of all comfort. Our job is not to defend God but rather to demonstrate God in a practical way. We must be channels of God's comfort to help people have the courage to face life honestly, the wisdom to understand what to do, the strength to do it, and the faith and hope to wait for God to do the rest. If we have experienced God's help in our own lives, we will have no problem sharing that help with others.

I ran across in my reading an old Gaelic saying that struck me as being applicable to our discussion on suffering. It says, "I, too, will turn my face to the wind, and cast my handful of seed on high."

When I read it, I thought of what Solomon wrote in Ecclesiastes 11:4, "Whoever watches the wind will not plant; whoever looks at the clouds will not reap."

Here are two opposite philosophies of life. One says, "This isn't a good day for sowing or reaping. The wind is blowing and a storm is brewing." The other says, "There never will be an ideal day for sowing or reaping. I'm not going to let the wind or the storm frighten me. I'll face the wind with courage and cast my handful of seed on high!"

And when you sow your seed, you never know where God will plant it and how He will use it to help others! It may seem like your efforts are "blowing in the wind," but God will see to it that they are not wasted.

There are plenty of "miserable comforters" in this world, people armed with threadbare clichés that only deepen our wounds instead of soothing them. Clichés like:

"Things could be worse," they tell us. *Could they? They seem pretty bad right now.*

"Other people have it worse than you do!" *Do they? How do you know? Anyway, should it make me feel better to know that others hurt worse than I do?*

"Just think of the wonderful memories you have!" *Have you ever tried to live on memories? Sometimes my past joys only magnify my present pain.*

Job had a good word for this kind of "comfort": "Your maxims are proverbs of ashes" (Job 13:12).

God's promises are medicine for the broken heart. Let Him comfort you. And, after He has comforted you, try to share that comfort with somebody else. It will do both of you good.

Dealing with Disaster

On May 25, 1979, American Airlines Flight #191 left O'Hare International Airport in Chicago, bound for Los Angeles. The DC-10 had hardly begun its ascent when it crashed to the ground, killing 275 passengers. We were living near O'Hare Field at that time and I recall how the announcement interrupted the baseball game and alerted all the viewers that an air disaster had occurred.

Not long after, I took Flight #191 to Los Angeles, and we had a fine trip. We flew over the scene of the crash, but you would never have known that anything tragic had taken place there. I understand that the airline has since "retired" Flight #191, giving it another number. Crew members and passengers were a bit uneasy about it.

Now that news coverage is so good, every disaster that takes place anywhere in the world is brought into our living room. We saw the funeral procession that carried the bodies of those forty-four French schoolchildren who were killed in the bus crash on July 31, 1982. We saw pictures of the boat that struck the bridge in Tampa Bay, and the cars that plunged into the water. "Instant disaster" is what we see, whether it's a storm in the Philippines, a school building fire in Chicago, or an explosion at a factory.

Sometimes the dramatic disasters cause us to forget the quiet tragedies. During one week in January 1982, the extremely cold weather caused the death of 230 persons in the United States. When people die in isolation, one at a time, they are local statistics; but when they die publicly in a group, they are part of a disaster. Sometimes our values are a bit out of balance. I suppose the thing that really disturbs us about a disaster is not so much the size of it, or even the suddenness, but the apparent *meaninglessness* of it. If forty-four soldiers are killed in an ambush, that is a part of war. But when forty-four children are killed while on a school trip, that raises questions that disturb us.

Hoping to embroil Jesus in a political argument, some people asked Him to comment on a recent tragedy in Jerusalem. Here is the text:

> Now there were some present at that time who told Jesus about the Galileans whose blood Pilate had mixed with their sacrifices. Jesus answered, "Do you think that these Galileans were worse sinners than all the other Galileans because they suffered this way? I tell you, no! But unless you repent, you too will all perish. Or those eighteen who died when the tower in Siloam fell on them—do you think they were more guilty than all the others living in Jerusalem? I tell you, no! But unless you repent, you too will all perish." Then he told this parable: "A man had a fig tree, planted in his vineyard, and he went to look for fruit on it,

but did not find any. So he said to the man who took care of the vineyard, 'For three years now I've been coming to look for fruit on this fig tree and haven't found any. Cut it down! Why should it use up the soil?' 'Sir,' the man replied, 'leave it alone for one more year, and I'll dig around it and fertilize it. If it bears fruit next year, fine! If not, then cut it down.'" (Luke 13:1–9)

Jesus didn't deny the fact that disasters do come to people. They come to religious people and to ordinary workmen on the job. They are caused by evil men, like Pilate, and by "acts of God" (or nature, depending on your belief) over which nobody has any control. But no matter what the cause or the circumstance, disasters leave empty places in homes and hearts. Both of these events described in Luke produced grieving widows, sorrowing parents, and crying children.

From our Lord's interpretation of these events, we can discover at least three warnings that we need to heed whenever a disaster occurs today.

To begin with, *we must be careful not to judge the victims.* It's so easy to conclude, "Well, somebody must have sinned and this was God's punishment!" Eliphaz would have looked at that charred and cluttered field near O'Hare and said, "Consider now: Who, being innocent, has ever perished?" (Job 4:7). The disciples might have asked, "Who sinned, these passengers or their parents, that they died in this crash?" (see John 9:1–2).

You and I are not to pass judgment on the victims of disasters. Only God knows their hearts. For that matter, godly people are also involved in these tragedies! How do we explain their death? There is no sense resurrecting Job's friends and setting up court. Disasters come to religious people in the temple and to busy people on the job, and only God knows all that is involved.

143

But not only must we not judge the victims, *we must not judge God*. Certainly God can prevent soldiers from murdering worshipers, or towers from falling on stonemasons. He can prevent school buses from getting involved in fatal accidents. He can stop airplanes from crashing. To be fair, you and I must confess that *nobody knows how many times God has done these things*. All we know about are the times when He did not.

We've been over this territory before, but we need to remind ourselves that God respects human freedom. Apart from freedom, there can be no character or true morality. Sometimes human freedom leads to error, and buses collide or planes crash; but God is certainly not to blame. He proves his sovereignty, not by intervening constantly and preventing these events, but by ruling and overruling them so that even tragedies end up accomplishing His ultimate purposes.

If God is responsible, then where does Pilate fit into the picture? Can Pilate excuse himself and say, "The Lord made me do it!" If this is the case, then we had better close all our courts because *nobody is guilty but God*.

"Then why didn't God change Pilate so he wouldn't be a murderer?" is the next question. I have no doubt that God would have been happy to see Pilate repent and live a godly life, but God will not force godly character on people. Forced morality is not morality at all. Once again, we are back to God's great respect for man's freedom of choice.

The startling warning that Jesus taught from these two events is this: *we ought to honestly judge ourselves!* The men who died in the temple and under the fallen tower were not greater sinners than we are—yet we're still alive! So, the major

144

question is not "Why did they die?" but rather "Why are you and I still alive?"

It is here that our Lord's parable comes in. I'm sure that He had the nation of Israel in mind when He told this story. He had ministered to them for three years, and yet the religious leaders had rejected Him. God in His mercy spared the nation and gave the people opportunity to repent.

But there is also a personal application: What good am I doing in God's world to prove that I'm fit to keep alive? Does He find fruit being produced from my life and ministry? If I were "cut down," would it make any difference to the work of God's kingdom in this world?

It's so easy to judge *others* in times of disaster. Psychiatrist Carl Jung has written, "Only a fool is interested in other people's guilt, since he cannot alter it. The wise man learns only from his own guilt." Being critical of others, including God, is a good way to avoid having to face and judge our own sins!

I may be wrong, but I have a feeling that many people react to so-called disasters in a shallow and temporary manner. No sooner is the news flash completed than the television viewers go right back to their baseball game, perhaps after saying, "That's too bad! Think of the people waiting in that Los Angeles airport!" Few of us will be so upset that we'll miss a meal or lose any sleep; and at coffee break the next day, we'll discuss the plane crash and the baseball game in the same breath.

So, I have a suspicion that much of the so-called debate among unbelievers about the disasters of life is simply cheap ammunition fired at the wrong target. It's an opportunity to blame God while, at the same time, they do little if anything to assist those who have been touched personally by the tragedy.

Finally, Jesus made it clear that the important thing is not *how* you die, but that you are *ready* to die. Can we be sure of life after life? Can we avoid death after death? This will be our topic in the next chapter, *the most important chapter in the entire book.*

Hope

Perhaps the two most familiar quotations on the theme of hope are Cicero's "While there's life, there's hope," and Alexander Pope's lines from *An Essay on Man*, published two centuries and a half ago:

> Hope springs eternal in the human breast:
> Man never is, but always to be blest.

Pope didn't really believe that it was necessary for us to know anything about the future. In fact, the less we know, the happier we might be. He wrote:

> Hope humbly then; with trembling pinions soar;
> Wait the great teacher Death, and God adore.

No wonder Pope wrote to his fellow poet John Gay what Pope called "the ninth beatitude": "Blessed is he who expects nothing, for he shall never be disappointed."

I seriously doubt that very many happy people live by this philosophy. "Everything that is done in the world is done by hope," said Martin Luther, and he is right. The farmer plants his seeds in hope, and the bride and groom plight their troth in hope. The three great virtues are faith, hope, and love. Faith reaches up to God, hope looks to the future, and love reaches out to those around us; and the three virtues belong together. Instead of saying, "Where there's life, there's hope," we ought to say, "Where there's *faith*, there's hope." "Hope is never ill," wrote John Bunyan, "when faith is well."

But true hope isn't just a fond wish that grips our hearts. True hope builds on a better foundation than "wishing will make it so." In his sentimental "Address At A Little Boy's Grave," the once-popular agnostic orator Robert Green Ingersoll said, "Help for the living, hope for the dead." But he never told us what the help was or how to get it, or what the foundation was for our hope.

To suffer without hope is to live in despair. Job had his ups and downs in this regard. "What strength do I have, that I should still hope?" he asked. "What prospects, that I should be patient?" (Job 6:11). "My days are swifter than a weaver's shuttle, and they come to an end without hope" (Job 7:6). Yet with a burst of faith, Job could say, "Though he slay me, yet will I hope in him" (Job 13:15).

Job used a striking image when he said, "He uproots my hope like a tree" (Job 19:10). A hope that is *rooted* is a hope that is alive and growing; but a hope that is *rooted up* is a dead hope. You can't nurture anything unless it has roots. Peter may have had this image in mind when he wrote to some suffering Christians: "Praise be to the God and Father of our Lord

Jesus Christ! In his great mercy he has given us new birth into a living hope through the resurrection of Jesus Christ from the dead" (1 Pet. 1:3). We have a living hope because we trust a living Savior!

To be sure, it's possible for the doctrine of a future life to become an opiate that lulls people into accepting the status quo (slavery, bad working conditions, cancer) and doing nothing about it. *But despair can be just as paralyzing.* My guess is that more people are genuinely motivated by hope than by hopelessness, and a part of that hope is the assurance of future glory with God for those who are His people.

One of our favorite places in London is the National Portrait Gallery. My wife and I have spent many happy and profitable hours looking at the portraits on display. Hebrews 11 is God's portrait gallery of the great heroes and heroines of the faith. What motivated Abraham, the founder of the Jewish nation? Or Moses, the liberator and lawgiver? Or the great conquerors like Joshua, Samson, and David? Or the great teachers and prophets like Samuel, Isaiah, and Daniel? *They were all motivated by a future hope.*

> All these people were still living by faith when they died. They did not receive the things promised; they only saw them and welcomed them from a distance. And they admitted that they were aliens and strangers on earth. People who say such things show that they are looking for a country of their own. If they had been thinking of the country they had left, they would have had opportunity to return. Instead, they were longing for a better country—a heavenly one. Therefore God is not ashamed to be called their God, for he has prepared a city for them. (Heb. 11:13–16)

These people were living in the future tense, and this gave them courage to make the most of the present. They were not fugitives running away from home, or vagabonds wishing they had a home. They were strangers on earth because they were away from home, and pilgrims because they were headed home. They were able to endure sacrifice, suffering, even death, because they knew where they were going.

One of the frequent Christian symbols found in the catacombs is the anchor. It's a symbol of hope. "We have this hope as an anchor for the soul, firm and secure" (Heb. 6:19). The Greek philosopher Epictetus said, "One must not tie a ship to a single anchor, nor life to a single hope." But God's people have always tied their lives to a single hope, the assurance of one day seeing God in heaven.

To Jesus Christ, heaven was not simply a destination; it was a motivation. As He faced the cross, He said, "The hour is come for the Son of Man to be glorified" (John 12:23). Glorified! I would have said "crucified." But Jesus looked beyond the suffering and saw the glory that would follow. The knowledge that He was going back to heaven was a strong motivation in His life. "Jesus knew that the time had come for him to leave this world and go to the Father. Having loved his own who were in the world, he now showed them the full extent of his love" (John 13:1).

Cicero said, "While there's life, there's hope." But Paul wrote, "If only for this life we have hope in Christ, we are to be pitied more than all men" (1 Cor. 15:19). As God's people, we don't say, "While there's life, there's hope." Instead we shout with confidence, "Because there is life in Christ, there is a living hope!"

The Harvard philosopher Alfred North Whitehead once asked a friend, "As for Christian theology, can you imagine anything more appallingly idiotic than the Christian idea of heaven?" With due respect for a brilliant man, I prefer to get my idea of heaven from Jesus Christ. This is what He said:

> Do not let your hearts be troubled. Trust in God; trust also in me. In my Father's house are many rooms; if it were not so, I would have told you. I am going there to prepare a place for you. And if I go and prepare a place for you, I will come back and take you to be with me that you also may be where I am. (John 14:1–3)

Jesus described heaven, not as the "court of an oriental despot" as Whitehead claimed, but as a home where a loving Father welcomed His children at the close of their journey. The apostle John added to the picture: "He [God] will wipe every tear from their eyes. There will be no more death or mourning or crying or pain, for the old order of things has passed away" (Rev. 21:4).

One of my favorite nature writers is Joseph Wood Krutch, whose books are beautifully written and filled with insight. But I can't agree with Krutch where he writes, "There is no reason to suppose that his [man's] own life has any more meaning than the life of the humblest insect that crawls from one annihilation to another." If the only future that man has is annihilation, why wait? Camus is right after all: The logical thing to do is commit suicide!

My pastoral ministry has put me in touch with people whose situation seemed hopeless from a human perspective, and yet they overcame their obstacles and handicaps and conquered in the end. Hope was not, for them, a distant prospect; it was an ever-present power. They imitated the attitude of Paul, who wrote, "I press on toward the goal to win the prize for which God has called me heavenward in Christ Jesus" (Phil. 3:14).

How does this future hope enable us to bear today's burdens and pain? *It assures us that we're not suffering in vain.* From a human point of view, as the Book of Ecclesiastes argues, life is but a series of disappointments and everything is "vanity." But not from the Christian point of view! Paul climaxed his great "resurrection chapter" with these words: "Therefore, my dear brothers, stand firm. Let nothing move you. Always give yourselves fully to the work of the Lord, because you know that your labor in the Lord is not in vain" (1 Cor. 15:58).

This means that God's people don't sacrifice and suffer in vain. Our present suffering is an investment in future glory. For us, heaven is not "pie in the sky by and by," the carrot on the string in front of the horse. We are citizens of heaven *here and now*, and we are sharing *now* the life of heaven within our hearts. Paul described our present experience perfectly in one of his benedictions: "May the God of hope fill you with all joy and peace as you trust in him, so that you may overflow with hope by the power of the Holy Spirit" (Rom. 15:13).

No matter what our philosophy of life may be, or what our religious beliefs, all of us face death. The world into which Jesus was born had no hope for life after death. The attitude of most people at that time is reflected in this epitaph:

> I was not.
> I was.
> I am not.
> I care not.

God's people would never use that kind of epitaph, because Jesus Christ "has destroyed death and has brought life and immortality to light through the gospel" (2 Tim. 1:10). He promised His disciples, "Because I live, you also will live" (John 14:19). For God's people, *life is not a dead-end street!*

Jesus not only conquered death, by His death and resurrection, but He even changed the meaning of death. For the believer, death is *sleep.* The body sleeps, but the spirit goes to be with the Lord. When Jesus Christ returns,

> the dead in Christ will rise first. After that, we who are still alive will be caught up with them in the clouds to meet the Lord in the air. And so we will be with the Lord forever. (1 Thess. 4:16–17)

Paul used an interesting word for death; he called it "departure" (2 Tim. 4:6). The Greek word is a military term: "taking down a tent and relocating." That's what death is for God's people, simply leaving behind the worn-out tent and going into better and more glorious quarters! It is also a naval term: "to hoist anchor and set sail." There will be no storms on that sea!

The farmers also used this term for "the unyoking of the oxen." Death for the believer means that the burdens are lifted and the work is finished. "Blessed are the dead who die in the Lord from now on," said a voice from heaven. The apostle John heard the reply: "'Yes,' says the Spirit, 'they will rest from their labor, for their deeds will follow them'" (Rev. 14:13).

While looking at the faded gravestones in an old cemetery, I found an epitaph that I had often heard quoted but had never seen for myself. Here it is:

Pause, my friend, as you go by.
As you are now, so once was I.
As I am now, so you will be.
Prepare, my friend, to follow me!

I understand that somebody added this footnote in one cemetery:

To follow you is not my intent,
Until I know which way you went!

We smile at this bit of doggerel, but it carries a powerful message and asks a pertinent question: "Where will you go when your life ends?" God's people know the answer: they go home to be with God forever.

"But, don't *all* good people go to heaven?" some may ask.

I must confess that the word *good* bothers me just a bit. We talk about bad things happening to "good people," and I'm just wondering who these "good people" are. Apparently it's permissible for bad things to happen to *bad* people, but not for bad things to happen to *good* people. I'm not sure who has the authority for deciding which of us is "bad" and which of us is "good."

Most of the believers I've had contact with have told me that God has been far better to them than they deserve, and this includes people who have suffered greatly. In fact, the great saints in both Judaism and Christianity have all confessed that they were undeserving sinners who depended entirely on the grace and mercy of God.

"I am nothing but dust and ashes," said Abraham to the Lord (Gen. 18:27). Job had a similar confession: "I despise myself and repent in dust and ashes" (Job 42:6). And listen to David:

"Surely I have been a sinner from birth" (Ps. 51:5). Isaiah the prophet was not ashamed to give his admission of guilt: "Woe to me! . . . I am ruined! For I am a man of unclean lips" (Isa. 6:5).

The apostle Peter said to Jesus, "Go away from me, Lord; I am a sinful man" (Luke 5:8). Even the mighty apostle Paul had no delusions about himself. He wasn't "playing to the grandstands" when he wrote: "Christ Jesus came into the world to save sinners—of whom I am the worst" (1 Tim. 1:15).

I know it sounds negative, and it certainly doesn't inflate anybody's ego, but the conclusion is this: "There is no one righteous, not even one. . . . There is no one who does good, not even one" (Rom. 3:10, 12).

In one of his books, the late Dr. D. Martyn Lloyd-Jones, who pastored for many years in London, discusses the difference between true salvation in Christ and mere religious morality. He points out that the merely "good person" likes to boast about his morality, while the Christian knows how sinful he is and that he must depend wholly on God's grace. He doesn't boast and he doesn't try to defend himself before God. "His mouth has been stopped," wrote Dr. Lloyd-Jones; and then he added, "Has your mouth ever been stopped?"

A very religious man, a leader in his faith, was browsing in the "Religion" section of the library and happened to take Dr. Lloyd-Jones's book from the shelf and begin to read it casually. He got to that penetrating question: "Has your mouth ever been stopped?" and it struck him with such force that he said in response, "Why, no, my mouth has never been stopped!" The more he pondered the matter, the more he realized that he was depending on his own self-righteousness and not on God's grace.

Before he put the book back on the shelf, the man had confessed to God that he was a sinner, that he wasn't good enough to get into heaven on his own, and that he needed the Savior. God met him in that library, and his life was transformed.

So, I would ask you the same question: "Has your mouth ever been stopped?"

Job's mouth was stopped. In all of his suffering, he felt God was giving him a "raw deal," and he longed for the opportunity to face God and defend himself. But when Job finally did face God, this was his defense: "I am unworthy—how can I reply to you? I put my hand over my mouth" (Job 40:4).

The worst thing that can happen to you is not the death of a loved one, a prolonged illness, or a painful accident. The worst thing that could happen to you would be to suffer *for nothing*, die, and be lost forever.

God's people suffer for something—for Someone—and when they die, they enter into heaven where all their investment of suffering is transformed into glory.

Has your mouth ever been stopped?

If it has, then you are a candidate for God's salvation. Open that mouth and ask Him to save you! God's promise is that "everyone who calls on the name of the Lord will be saved" (Joel 2:32; Acts 2:21).

Questions You May Be Asking

Whenever I have preached on the subject of suffering, people have come to me afterward to ask me about things that have perplexed them. Sometimes they brought the question with them to the meeting, but often the matter was raised by something I said in the sermon. Some of these questions are included here because they are typical of the problems that thinking people have with their religious faith.

Let me make it clear that the central thesis of this book (and my ministry) is that we live by promises, not by explanations. However, this should not prevent us from using the minds God has given us and seeking to understand His thoughts after Him. "The secret things belong to the LORD our God," Moses told the people of Israel, "but the things revealed belong to us and to our children forever, that we may follow all the words of this law" (Deut. 29:29). God does not reveal truth to the curious, but to the serious, those who are willing to obey it.

Q. *It's comforting to know that God suffers with us, but I'm not sure I understand what that means. I always thought that God was above suffering and lived in eternal bliss.*

A. Whenever we talk about God, we have to use human language and begin with what we know. The words we use to "describe" God are not the same as the very nature of God. All language has its limitations, but better to use a limited language than not to know God at all.

When human beings think of the term *suffering*, we relate it usually to *physical* pain. God doesn't have a body, because God is spirit; so physical pain is out of the question. However, mature people know that the greatest pain is not always physical. A broken heart can hurt far worse than a broken leg. There is a "spiritual suffering" of the inner person that is just as real as the pain we feel in the body.

God *identifies* with us in our suffering. He doesn't ignore us or judge us. One reason Jesus Christ suffered as He did while on earth was that He might be prepared to assist us from heaven in our times of need (Heb. 2:14–18 and 4:15, 16). He understands just how we feel, and He feels with us.

The fact that God doesn't change need not pose a problem. God is not the "prisoner" of His divine attributes. He is free and sovereign and able to act, relate to us, and respond to us as He desires. In His essence, His being, God cannot change; but in His relations with creation, creatures, and man, God exercises freedom.

Because God is perfect, He lives in perfect joy; but this doesn't prevent Him from entering into the trials and tears of your life.

In fact, one reason that He identifies with your sorrow is that He might give you His joy. Sorrow and joy are not enemies. The greater joy you experience, the greater the possibility for sorrow. But the one doesn't negate the other. Jesus was a "man of sorrows" and yet was also eminently joyful.

The mystery of God's being, no philosopher or theologian can penetrate this side of heaven. The words we use are inadequate, but we have no other words. The Bible states that God identifies with His people when they hurt, and we have to accept this revelation whether we fully understand it or not. "In all their distress he too was distressed" (Isa. 63:9). He is near us when we suffer, and He understands our feelings. When we pray, He is sensitive to what we say. This, to me, is a great encouragement; and I wouldn't permit the difficulty of understanding the concept to rob me of the comfort of practicing the truth of it.

Q. *Why must innocent infants and children suffer?*
A. Because they are a part of the human race, and the human race (thanks to Adam) is conceived and born in sin. Paul discusses this important doctrine in Romans 5. He explains that Adam was the head of the human race, so that the entire race was on trial in Adam. When Adam fell, the whole race fell in him.

However, this approach makes possible our salvation. Jesus Christ came as the Head of a new race! In His death and resurrection, Jesus Christ not only undid all that Adam did, but He accomplished much more. Now all who believe in Jesus Christ are forgiven of their sins, made righteous in Jesus Christ, and made a part of God's "new creation" in Christ (2 Cor. 5:17).

Babies are conceived in sin (Ps. 51:5) and are born with a sinful nature. This means they are susceptible to all the ravages of sin that are a part of our "groaning" creation (Rom. 8:18–22). We thank God for all that medical science is doing to assure babies of normal births, and we ought to encourage this research as much as possible. However, we are fallen people in a fallen world, and there are still possibilities for tragedies and heartbreaks.

I might add that the greatest tragedies I've witnessed in my own ministry are not those that *can't* be explained, but those that *can* be explained. When immature young people have infected their bodies with venereal disease or toxic drugs, and then have brought malformed or malfunctioning babies into the world, you can't help but feel sorry for the babies. Nobody can "blame God" for these consequences.

When babies die, they go to heaven. When King David's infant son died, David said, "Can I bring him back again? I will go to him, but he will not return to me" (2 Sam. 12:23). Where was David going ultimately? "I will dwell in the house of the LORD forever" (Ps. 23:6).

It does seem cruel that innocent little ones should suffer as they do, but we have to believe that God is in control and knows what He is doing. God is certainly not to blame for the evil that sinful men and women bring upon their children, and Jesus spoke some scathing words against such people (Matt. 18:1–10).

Q. *Your approach to suffering seems so defeatist! You want us just to give in and not fight back! I disagree with that approach.*

A. If I gave you the impression that I'm asking suffering people to give in and give up, then I'm very sorry; because that's not the approach I recommend at all, nor is it the approach taught in the Bible. When suffering comes, we have to fight back—but we must be careful to fight the right enemy, using the right weapons, and for the right purpose.

As I mentioned in chapter 8, acceptance of suffering is not the same as resignation. *Acceptance is a part of the "fighting back."* We are saying to the Lord, "I accept the challenge! You and I will together turn this suffering into a servant, not a master." *Resignation* is a passive thing; it's the signal that we've given up. But *acceptance* is active; it's the signal that we are trusting God to give us the grace we need to turn seeming tragedy into triumph.

Suppose we decide to "fight back" in the usual sense of the term. Which enemy do we fight first? The pain? The seeming futility of the experience? The doctors? God? It's been my experience that my greatest enemy is *myself*! Until I get victory over myself, I'm in no condition to declare war on anybody or anything else!

No, the Christian approach to suffering (which I described in chapter 8) is not a defeatist attitude at all. It's an approach that demands the greatest amount of faith and courage, because you aren't thinking about yourself—you're thinking about the glory of God and the good of others.

Q. *What if a person isn't a "courageous soul" with a lot of faith? How do you handle "bad things"?*

A. You start right where you are. One of the great things about the Christian faith is that Jesus accepts us just as we are. We don't have to qualify to know Him! Just honestly admit what you are and where you are, and ask Him to make you what He wants you to be. The "great saints" of history didn't start at the top. They all started somewhere near the bottom and let God develop their faith and character. Remember, it's not the *strength* of your faith that's important. It's the *object* of your faith. If you are trusting God, then you will receive all that God can give you.

Q. *A friend of mine claims that there is "healing in the atonement," and that every Christian has the right to claim healing and perfect health because of the cross. Do you agree with this?*

A. No, I don't agree, and for several reasons. To begin with, this teaching is contradicted by experience. Paul had his thorn in the flesh, yet he was a dedicated believer. Timothy apparently had stomach problems (1 Tim. 5:23), and Epaphroditus almost died in Rome when he was ministering to Paul (Phil. 2:25–30). Paul commended Epaphroditus for his devotion, so we can't say he was sick because of his disobedience or lack of faith. I've been a student of Christian biography for many years, and I can affirm to you that many great servants of God suffered physical afflictions, and yet served God faithfully.

I reject this teaching also on doctrinal grounds. The Scripture that is usually cited to prove "healing in the atonement" is Isaiah 53:4–6. Certainly when Christ died on the cross, He died for our sins, and he bore the consequences of our sins. This salvation that He purchased includes the assurance of a glorified body one day in heaven (Phil. 3:20–21). But we don't have that glorified body yet; we're still "groaning" in the present body (Rom. 8:22–23).

If physical healing *now* is a part of our salvation, then every sinner who trusts Christ would instantly be healed of whatever illnesses and handicaps he suffered, and this just doesn't happen.

The "healing" referred to in Isaiah 53:5 ("and by his wounds we are healed") is primarily *spiritual*—the sickness of sin. At least this is the way Peter interpreted it (1 Pet. 2:21–24).

Finally, I reject this teaching because it leads to confusion and despair. When people expect God to do something that He hasn't promised to do, they eventually become bitter—or renounce their faith—when God doesn't live up to His "promise." If healing is a part of the atonement, and I claim that healing but don't receive it, *then perhaps I never really received the atonement either!* I may yet be a lost sinner! You can see the problems that could develop.

Let me add this: this teaching of "healing in the atonement" agrees with the philosophy of Satan and Job's friends. It puts a greater premium on the physical than on the spiritual. "Does Job fear God for nothing?" People would trust Christ, not because they are lost sinners who need to be saved, but because they want to get well!

It's worth noting that Matthew applied Isaiah 53:4 to our Lord's *ministry on earth* (Matt. 8:14–17). When Jesus healed the sick, He was bearing their afflictions, not in a substitutionary sense but as the Healer. Jesus had not yet died on the cross, yet Matthew applied Isaiah 53:4 to His ministry!

Ultimate healing and the glorification of the body are certainly among the blessings of Calvary for the believing Christian. *Immediate* healing is not guaranteed. God *can* heal any disease—except the last one!—but He is not obligated to do so.

Q. *What about the Holocaust?*
A. I'm not sure what you are referring to in your question. Do you mean, "Why did it occur?" or, "Why didn't God stop it?"

There have always been tragedies in history, and the Holocaust is one of the greatest. The principles I discuss in chapter 11 apply here. The big question is not, "Why did six million Jews die?" but "Why are you and I still alive?"

Certainly the Holocaust reveals the wickedness of the human heart. The optimistic humanist has a tough time explaining why it happened. Instead of blaming God, we need to turn to God and repent! I would hope that the tragedy of the Holocaust would be a constant reminder to mankind that education, science, and even religion do not make a nation morally upright. There must be a living faith in God. The people who perpetrated the Holocaust were the heirs of the Reformation!

The worst judgment God can bring on an individual or a nation is to permit them to have their own way. The commentary on this is found in Romans 1:18–32, and I recommend that you ponder it.

Q. *How can I best prepare for any tragedies that might come to me or my loved ones?*

A. By trusting Christ and walking with Him day by day. By spending time in His Word so that your faith is a dynamic thing, growing and reaching out to others. By building enriching relationships with your family and friends. By trusting God in the "little problems" of life, and seeing Him work things out.

But let me add this warning: Don't adopt a fearful and pessimistic attitude toward life! If you are *afraid* of life, you'll start to create your own problems whether you want to or not! "God is love. Whoever lives in love lives in God, and God in him. . . . There is no fear in love. But perfect love drives out fear" (1 John 4:16, 18).

Face life with a zestful spirit! God has great things planned for His children. Your Father always prepares *you* for what He prepares *for you*, so stay close to Him. Serve others and help to bear their burdens. You'll be ready if suffering comes, and God will see you through.

A Little Anthology

Over the years, in my reading and personal ministry, I have discovered some choice statements of spiritual and philosophical truth that have helped me a great deal. Whenever I have shared them, in counseling or preaching, they have seemed to help others. I share them now with you.

Ah, if you knew what peace there is in an accepted sorrow!

Madame Guyon

It is a greater thing to pray for pain's conversion than its removal.

P. T. Forsythe

Make friends with your trials, as though you were always to live together.

St. Francis de Sales

It is faith's work to claim and challenge lovingkindnesses out of all the roughest strokes of God.

Samuel Rutherford

We must leave to God all that depends on Him, and think only of being faithful in all that depends upon ourselves.

François Fénelon

You cannot cure your sorrow by nursing it; but you can cure it by nursing another's sorrow.

George Matheson

There is no profit in walking mournfully. All the profit a man ever gets is from his joy. The advantages of the fires of sorrow do not lie in the things they consume. The sweetest of all the uses of adversity is to show me the joy which it cannot take away.

George Matheson

The God of Israel, the Savior, is sometimes a God that hides Himself, but never a God that absents Himself; sometimes in the dark, but never at a distance.

Matthew Henry

No man ever sank under the burden of the day. It is when tomorrow's burden is added to the burden of today, that the weight is more than a man can bear. Never load yourselves so. If you find yourselves loaded, at least remember this: it is your doing, and not God's. He begs you to leave the future to Him and mind the present.

George MacDonald

In perplexities—when we cannot tell what to do, when we cannot understand what is going on around us—let us be calmed and steadied and made patient by the thought that what is hidden from us is not hidden from Him.

Frances Ridley Havergal

Never fancy you could be something if only you had a different lot and sphere assigned to you. The very things that you most deprecate, as fatal limitations or obstructions, are probably what you most want. What you call hindrances, obstacles, discouragements, are probably God's opportunities.

Horace Bushnell

You don't have to search for God; you have only to realize Him.

Gerhart Tersteegen

Think and care in no wise about what is to come. Love and suffer in the present moment, thinking more about God and His strength than of yourself and your weakness. If increase of suffering comes, increase of grace will come also.

Gerhart Tersteegen

Suffering without love is for the damned; love with suffering is for the blessed. Here on earth, we honor God by both, as children of love, crucified.

Gerhart Tersteegen

As long as we want to be different from what God wants us to be at the time, we are only tormenting ourselves to no purpose.

Gerhart Tersteegen

I do not pray for a lighter load, but for a stronger back.

Phillips Brooks

All I have seen teaches me to trust the Creator for all I have not seen.

Ralph Waldo Emerson

A little faith will bring your soul to heaven, but a lot of faith will bring heaven to your soul.

Dwight L. Moody

God judged it better to bring good out of evil than to suffer no evil to exist.

St. Augustine

Where your pleasure is, there is your treasure; where your treasure, there your heart; where your heart, there your happiness.

St. Augustine

Despise not thy school of sorrow, O my soul; it will give thee a unique part in the universal song.

George Matheson

God gave burdens, also shoulders.

Yiddish Proverb

Joys impregnate; sorrows bring forth.

William Blake

Suffering is closely connected with freedom. To seek a life in which there will be no more suffering is to seek a life in which there will be no more freedom.

Nikolai Berdyaev

For what is prayer? To connect every thought with the thought of God. To look on everything as His work and His appointment. To submit every thought, wish, and resolve to Him. To feel His presence so that it shall restrain us even in our wildest joy. That is prayer.

Frederick W. Robertson

Our suffering is not worthy [of] the name of suffering. When I consider my crosses, tribulations, and temptations, I shame myself almost to death, thinking what are they in comparison of the sufferings of my blessed Savior Jesus Christ.

Martin Luther

The truest help we can render an afflicted man is not to take his burden from him, but to call out his best strength that he may be able to bear the burden.

Phillips Brooks

Why should I tremble at the plough of my Lord, that maketh deep furrows in my soul? I know He is no idle husbandman; He purposeth a crop.

Samuel Rutherford

Adversity is the diamond dust Heaven polishes its jewels with.

Robert Leighton

One Son God has without sin, but none without sorrow.

John Trapp

We may feel God's hand as a Father upon us when He strikes us as well as when He strokes us.

Abraham Wright

O how many have been coached to hell in the chariots of earthly pleasures, while others have been whipped to heaven by the road of affliction!

John Flavel

Encouragement from the Scriptures

Will not the Judge of all the earth do right?

Abraham (Genesis 18:25)

The eternal God is your refuge, and underneath are the everlasting arms.

Moses (Deuteronomy 33:27)

Have I not commanded you? Be strong and courageous. Do not be terrified; do not be discouraged, for the LORD your God will be with you wherever you go.

Joshua 1:9

Even though I walk through the valley of the shadow of death, I will fear no evil, for you are with me; your rod and your staff, they comfort me.

Psalm 23:4

Why are you so downcast, my soul? Why so disturbed within me? Put your hope in God, for I will yet praise him, my Savior and my God.

Psalm 42:11

You will keep in perfect peace him whose mind is steadfast, because he trusts in you.

Isaiah 26:3

So do not fear, for I am with you; do not be dismayed, for I am your God. I will strengthen you and help you; I will uphold you with my righteous right hand.

Isaiah 41:10

When you pass through the waters, I will be with you; and when you pass through the rivers, they will not sweep over you. When you walk through the fire, you will not be burned; the flames will not set you ablaze. For I am the LORD, your God, the Holy One of Israel, your Savior.

Isaiah 43:2–3

"Though the mountains be shaken and the hills be removed, yet my unfailing love for you will not be shaken nor my covenant of peace be removed," says the LORD, who has compassion on you.

Isaiah 54:10

Come to me, all you who are weary and burdened, and I will give you rest. Take my yoke upon you and learn from me, for I am gentle and humble in heart, and you will find rest for your souls. For my yoke is easy and my burden is light.

Jesus (Matthew 11:28–30)

Warren W. Wiersbe has served as a pastor, Bible teacher, and seminary instructor and is the author of more than 150 books, including the popular BE series of Bible expositions. He pastored the Moody Church in Chicago and also ministered with Back to the Bible Broadcast for ten years, five of them as Bible teacher and general director. His conference ministry has taken him to many countries. He and his wife, Betty, make their home in Lincoln, Nebraska, where he continues his writing ministry.

EXPERIENCE MORE SATISFYING AND EFFECTIVE PRAYER.

HOW THE LORD'S PRAYER TEACHES
US TO PRAY MORE EFFECTIVELY

ON EARTH AS IT IS IN HEAVEN

WARREN W. WIERSBE

978-0-8010-7219-2

Do you feel like your prayer life is stagnant? Like you're saying the same things to God that you did when you first started praying?

Just as young children slowly learn to communicate in more and more complex ways, so Christians should move from simply crying out to God to a mature, developed prayer life. The basic elements found in the Lord's Prayer are a helpful guide to believers hoping to enrich their prayers.

In *On Earth as It Is in Heaven*, beloved teacher and writer Warren Wiersbe explains and applies the elements of the Lord's Prayer so you can reach new levels of maturity in your own personal prayer life.

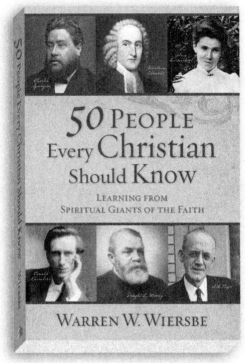

CPSIA information can be obtained at www.ICGtesting.com
Printed in the USA
BVOW04s1430090816

458452BV00001B/1/P